Dreams and Miracles

Other Books by Ann Spangler

An Angel a Day: Stories of Angelic Encounters
A Miracle a Day: Stories of Heavenly Encounters

Dreams and Miracles

How God Speaks Through Your Dreams

Previously published as *Dreams*

ANN SPANGLER

ZondervanPublishingHouse

Grand Rapids, Michigan

A Division of HarperCollinsPublishers

Dreams and Miracles
Copyright © 1997 by Ann Spangler

Previously published as *Dreams*

Requests for information should be addressed to:

ZondervanPublishingHouse
Grand Rapids, Michigan 49530

Library of Congress Cataloging-in-Publication Data

Spangler, Ann.
    [Dreams]
    Dreams and miracles: how God speaks through your dreams / Ann Spangler.
       p.   cm.
    Includes bibliographical references.
    ISBN: 0-310-22907-3 (hardcover)
    1. Dreams—Religious aspects—Christianity.   2. Spiritual life—Christianity.   I. Title.
    BR115.D74S63   1999
    248.2'9—dc21   98-42789
                                                               CIP

This edition printed on acid-free paper and meets the American National Standards
Institute Z39.48 standard.

All Scripture quotations, unless otherwise indicated, are taken from the *Holy Bible: New
International Version*®. NIV®. Copyright © 1973, 1978, 1984 by International Bible
Society. Used by permission of Zondervan Publishing House. All rights reserved.

Published in association with Wolgemuth and Associates, Inc., 330 Franklin Road #135A-106,
Brentwood, TN 37027

Printed in the United States of America

---

99 00 01 02 03 04 /❖ DC/ 10 9 8 7 6 5 4 3 2 1

To Beth Feia

Encouragement Is a Rare Gift
Thank You for Sharing It So Generously

$\mathscr{C}$ONTENTS ๛

$\mathcal{A}$CKNOWLEDGMENTS ↔

$\mathcal{T}$his book would never have been written were it not for Michelle Rapkin and Barbara Greenman, whose creativity provided the spark for investigating whether our dreams can sometimes offer windows that link us to spiritual realities. To them both I am profoundly grateful.

I am also indebted to all whose stories are told in the following pages. In each case, these men and women were willing to share the intimate details of their dreams in hopes of helping others recognize the variety of ways in which God communicates. In a few cases, the names of those whose stories are told have been disguised to protect their privacy.

Special thanks also go to Charlene Ann Baumbich, Tracy Danz, Ken Gire, Donna Huisjen, Mary Ann Leland, LaVonne Neff, Elizabeth Newenhuyse, John Topliff, and Hendrika Vande Kemp for suggesting individuals whose stories might be right for the book. I am also grateful to Sandy Vander Zicht, my acquiring editor at Zondervan, who, from the beginning, caught the vision for this book. Bob Hudson, as always, deserves kudos for his encouragement, diplomacy, and editorial acumen. Scott Bolinder, more than once, provided support and help when I needed it most. Thanks also to Robert Wolgemuth, my agent, for his efforts on my behalf.

Earth is crammed full of heaven,

and every common bush aglow with God.

Those who see take off their shoes. . .

—ROBERT BROWNING

One

~

We Are Dreamers
Every One

*The price for denying the supernatural is cynicism, the scornful,
smug rejection of testimony from others who report their observations
of a world other and greater than that in which we ordinarily live.
The literature of mankind—biography, history, fiction, poetry,
theology—is permeated with intimations of things unseen.*

—MARY MCDERMOTT SHIDELER

I have always marveled at our ability to tell ourselves stories while we sleep, for that is the essence of dreaming. Each night we become the main character in some fantastic new drama. In a corner of our brains we keep a closet full of props—thousands of colorful images and insights that we drag out each night to tell the story. It is wonderful to be so gifted.

The novelist Reynolds Price talks about dreams as the art of the artless, pointing out that "people who don't write poetry, choreograph, paint pictures, whatever, do in fact, every night when they're asleep, construct works of art in their heads. The constructs usually turn out to be as impermanent as snowmen; but whatever dreams are about, they do seem to be everybody's attempt at, among other things, constructing storylike pieces of art."

It would be fascinating to pick and choose among such nightly dramas to retell dreams that conveyed a spiritual story. Does God sometimes try to catch our attention through such stories? Is it easier to get through to us when our daytime defenses are down? Is the veil between the supernatural and the natural world somehow thinner while we sleep, or does it only seem so? Kelly Bulkeley raises this issue in his book *Spiritual Dreaming:* "Woody Allen once said, 'There is no question that there is an unseen world. The problem is how far is it from midtown and how late is it open?'" The answer, says Bulkeley, is that "the 'unseen world' is as close as our pillows and it's open twenty-four hours a day."

When I first considered the possibility of writing a book about the spiritual nature of dreams, the idea both fascinated and unnerved me. Like anyone else, I have had my share of embarrassing, enlightening, frightening, and even wonderful dreams. Some of these have moved me to tears and others to hilarious laughter. Occasionally they have yielded startling insights. Rarely have they bored me.

Still such an undertaking seemed perilous. Most of the books about dreams I had encountered were shelved in New Age sections of local bookstores. Was the subject of dreams appropriate only to writers with more eclectic spiritual beliefs than mine? Or should dreams rather be left to scientists, armed with facts and figures, experts in black and white who could tell us what to make of something so nebulous? Was it wiser for most of us to ignore our dreams in hopes they would evaporate with the morning sun and trouble us no more?

Once the subject was introduced, I couldn't stop thinking of all the marvelous dreams I had read in Scripture. There was Abraham, who dreamed of a sacrifice, a flame, and a covenant with the living God. Abimelech, who was warned in a dream not to covet another man's wife. Jacob dreaming of angels. Joseph's dream of the sun and moon and eleven stars bowing down to him. Pharaoh's dream of seven years of plenty and seven years of famine. Solomon's dream of obtaining wisdom. Daniel, the great interpreter of dreams. The Magi's dream warning the three kings to evade Herod on their eastward journey. Joseph's dream directing him to flee to Egypt with Mary and the child Jesus.

The Bible, in fact, often speaks of dreams and visions as though they are the same, sometimes referring to dreams as "visions of the night." It seems unlikely that Scripture would contain such accounts if dreams were forbidden territory for people of faith.

A Word to the Wise

By pointing out that Scripture is full of dreams of a spiritual nature, I do not, of course, mean to elevate the testimony of our dreams to that of Scripture. Dreams are only one source of insight, which must be balanced by what we already know of God and his Word. It would be foolish to make a major decision solely on the basis of a dream. If our dreams urge us in a direction contrary to the laws of God, the laws of the nation, or the basic law of love that should govern us, then we have taken a wrong turn.

Furthermore, the father of modern dream analysis, Carl Jung, himself, warned that paying too much attention to dreams could make matters worse for an unbalanced person: "There are some people whose mental condition is so unbalanced that the interpretation of their dreams can be extremely risky; in such a case, a very one-sided consciousness is cut off from a correspondingly irrational or 'crazy' unconscious, and the two should not be brought together without taking special precautions."

In fact, dreams are a subjective landscape in which mountains and molehills are easily confused. Making sense of them is more an art than a science.

To make matters worse, our dreams are affected by a variety of factors: what we eat, whether we are well or ill, the temperature of the room in which we are sleeping, events of the previous day, and even, perhaps, malicious influences that at times harass us.

Why then should we bother about our dreams? Because our dreams can provide insights that often elude us in our waking lives. They can protect us from danger. Divert us from a wrong course. Show us how to pray. Hold a mirror to our souls. Help us say good-bye. They can even be a source of healing.

So, I have decided to wade into deep waters and write a book about dreams, even though I am not an expert in this field. What was the turning point for me? My decision was made once I became convinced that ignoring our dreams puts us at risk of ignoring God—limiting his influence as the Creator of our minds, emotions, bodies, and souls. Who are we, I wondered, to tell God he can visit us only while our eyes are open? When we diminish God's role in our lives, I believe we diminish our souls as well. Available grace may be withdrawn. The word spoken may be hushed beyond hearing. Of course, God is free to find another way, but why make it so difficult?

Not long after I reached my turning point, I came across a comment made by Charles Haddon Spurgeon, one of the nineteenth century's most eminent preachers, in a sermon regarding a dream he had: "We must take care that we do not neglect heavenly monitions through fear of being considered visionary . . . for to stifle a thought from God is no small sin." And then there was John Calvin's evenhanded comment: "Even profane writers very correctly consider dreams connected with divine agency. Yet, it would be foolish to extend this to all dreams." There is also the stirring prophecy of Joel in the Old Testament, assuring us that "your old men will dream dreams and your young men will see visions." And the book of Job says: "For God does speak— now one way, now another—though man may not perceive it. In a dream, in a vision of the night, when deep sleep falls on men as they slumber in their beds, he may speak in their ears."

Certainly, I do not believe every dream contains a message from God. I confess I have never kept a journal of my dreams, nor have I scrutinized many of my dreams to find their hidden meaning. I am like most people who occasionally have a dream that seems rather extraordinary. The dream is vivid. It troubles or fascinates me. These are the ones I pay attention to.

Regardless of whether I pay attention to them, I believe all dreams have a purpose, though not necessarily a spiritual one. To quote the poet Maya Angelou: "I do believe dreams have a function. I don't see anything that has no function, not anything that has been created. I may not understand its function or be able to even use it, . . . but I believe it has a reason. The brain is so strange and wondrous in its mystery. I think it creates a number of things for itself—it creates launching places and resting places—and it lets steam off and it reworks itself."

I hope you will find it refreshing to travel with me as a fellow pilgrim, seeking answers and insights by listening to the stories of people whose dreams have deepened their spiritual lives. As I see it, my task as both writer and pilgrim is to take the Scriptures seriously, letting them form a secure foundation as I listen to the stories of those who have experienced God working through their dreams. As such, I am a reporter of dreams rather than an interpreter of them. Those whose stories I tell are the only ones who can explain the meaning of their dreams.

In the process, I hope to help you become more sensitive to the ways God might be working in your own dreams. As in any endeavor, it is good to proceed with a measure of caution, asking God for wisdom, which is often a matter of finding balance between extremes. We do well neither to ignore our dreams nor to fixate on them.

In fact our dreams are a lot like our emotions. Both are gifts from God though they may not always seem so. Both can be tools, either of blessing or evil in our lives. The closer we are to God, the more we will find our dreams and our feelings reflecting his presence.

Most of the stories in this book came through that powerful research tool called "word of mouth." In fact, it surprised me how easy it was to unearth them once people knew what I was looking for. I heard from friends and friends of friends. That explains why a disproportionate number are from writers. I have even had the temerity to share a few of my own dreams. But there are many others—a mother, a high school student, a firefighter, a salesperson, a grandmother, a nurse, a psychology professor, a baseball enthusiast, a businessman— a few of whom wrote to me after seeing a notice in one of three publications, requesting stories from those who had had dreams of unusual spiritual significance.

It also surprised me that so many of the dreams recounted were negative dreams: nightmares or frustrating dreams that ended up having a positive effect on the dreamer. These too were seen as gifts from God.

In each case, I interviewed people by phone in order to include their stories in the book. I refrained from using stories from those whose credibility was difficult to ascertain or from others who could recount their dreams but not tell me what they meant. Many other stories were not used because they were so similar to ones I had already chosen.

A Few Pointers

*Y*ou may appreciate a few pointers before plunging into the stories that follow. By understanding some basic information about dreams, I hope your insights about your own dreams will be richer as well. Of course, these brief comments merely skim the surface of all that could be said about dreams. I have only noted points that were helpful to me as I listened to the dream stories recounted by people across the country.

1. In 1953 researchers discovered REM (Rapid Eye Movement) sleep, in which our eyes move rapidly beneath our lids, as though we are viewing a scene in a movie. Our most vivid dreams occur during REM sleep.

2. Though some people are convinced they never dream, each of us spends about one-fifth of our sleeping hours immersed in dreams. That means five years of our lives are spent dreaming. The activity of dreaming is so important that being deprived of it can result in a mental breakdown, even a psychotic break.

3. If a dream strikes you as particularly important, write it down as soon as you wake up or else you will probably forget it. Unless you have been in the habit of ignoring and repressing your dreams, you will probably know when a dream is significant.

4. Our dreams are always right about what we are feeling, but they are not necessarily objectively true. For instance, you may have a

dream that someone you love is killed in an accident. Chances are, that person will live another thirty years. Your dream may indicate you are worried about that person's reckless lifestyle. Your perception that they are headed for destruction may or may not be accurate. But that is how you are feeling about it.

5. It matters what we *do* in response to our dreams, not how creatively or frequently we interpret them. If God is speaking, we need to respond.

6. Dreams tell stories through the use of symbols. Unlike signs, which are one-dimensional, a symbol is multidimensional. Symbols are objects, people, words, things familiar to us in our daily life that take on much larger meaning in our dreams. For instance, roller-blading on a sidewalk is not a remarkable activity, at least if you're under twenty-five. But if you dream you are roller-blading on a freeway, your dream may be trying to tell you that you are engaging in some kind of risky and irresponsible behavior. It may be warning you to stop, before you suffer a nasty accident.

7. Dreams often have layers of meaning. You may recognize one aspect of your dream but be oblivious to others.

8. Dreams often have multiple functions: spiritual, psychological, and physiological. Some of them merely involve clearing the clutter in our minds. They help us to review, reorganize, and comment on the events of our daily life.

9. Most dreams tell a story, in which you are the main character. Strange as it sounds, you can be more than one person in your dream. The different characters may reflect different aspects of your personality. By reflecting on the way the characters act and react to each other you may discover some interesting things about yourself, perhaps raising issues you don't feel comfortable dealing with in your waking life.

Of course, not every character in your dream is you in disguise. If you dream about your mother, for instance, you may really be dreaming about your mother rather than the motherly aspects of yourself. In this way, dreams can be a mirror to your soul, reflecting problems and issues as well as progress you are making in humility, forgiveness, trust, generosity, and other virtues. As Robert Van de Castle has pointed out, "We are not hypocrites in our dreams."

10. Pay attention to how your dream made you feel. Were you sad, frightened, astonished, happy, peaceful, embarrassed? These feelings are a clue to what is really going on. For instance, if you dream a friend has died, but you are not troubled, it may be worth taking a closer look at the dream.

11. Pay attention to colors in your dreams. Contrary to popular belief, most of us do dream in color. Red could be a sign of passion or anger, green could represent envy or new life. Colors can represent different things to different people, so don't be dogmatic.

12. In dreams, a house usually represents the dreamer, while individual rooms in the house represent aspects of the dreamer's life or personality. Notice the style of the architecture and the size of the house and its rooms. How old is the house? Is it well cared for or has it fallen into disrepair? These kinds of questions can provide clues to what is happening in your life.

13. Cars too can be a symbol for you and where you may be heading. Who is driving, how fast is the car going, and is it under control?

14. Despite my comments about houses, cars, and colors, avoid using dream dictionaries. One writer compares them to horoscopes rather than to objective sources of knowledge about our dreams. Though it seems true that some symbols convey fairly universal meaning, symbols cannot be separated from the person who dreams them.

The symbols that surface in our dreams reflect our uniqueness as individuals. Don't make the mistake of treating dreams as though they are secret codes to be cracked.

15. A recurring dream usually signals that you are not getting the message. Resist the temptation to roll over in bed and, instead, ask yourself what the dream might be trying to tell you.

16. Most of us wake up before our nightmares are over. Our fear wakes us. A nightmare acts as an alarm, whose purpose is to "wake us up" to something we need to face. A recurring nightmare is an even stronger sign you are dealing with unresolved issues. George Howe Colt, in a recent article in *Life* magazine, helps explain the function of nightmares: "If dreams are an emotional thermostat, nightmares indicate that something is boiling over. Most people have only one or two a year. Psychiatrist Ernest Hartmann believes those who have more tend to be people who are especially sensitive and trusting, who tend toward creative professions like the arts, teaching, and—surprise—psychotherapy."

17. Some dreams are compensatory in nature. In other words, they may compensate for feelings we are having in our waking life. For instance, if you have been on your high horse lately, you might dream of falling off a roof. You may be sensing your need for more humility, lest pride set you up for a fall. Or if you repeatedly dream you are a great basketball star despite the fact that you can hardly throw a ball through the hoop, you may be compensating for feelings of inadequacy. Though dreams of falling and flying may be compensatory, flying dreams may also signal feelings of freedom or spiritual transcendence.

∽

Every evening, millions of people lie down to sleep, little suspecting they will soon take center stage in dramas of their own creating. On waking, such dream stories normally appear fantastic, funny, or all-too-forgettable. Occasionally, though, the effect will linger, stirring a longing, awakening a forgotten hunger, disturbing our complacency, causing us to wonder whether another, more creative Dramatist might also have been at work in the middle of the night.

The stories that follow tell of such dreams. They have been gathered into thematic sections, depending on the nature of the message—dreams that glimpse the future, that offer guidance, that bring healing, that provide wisdom, that resolve our grief, or that beckon us into deeper relationship with the One who made us dreamers in the first place—these are the dreams, the stories that shape our lives.

Two

❧

Dreaming the Future

"It is the charm of dreams that they introduce us into a
new infinity. Time and space are annihilated, gravity is
suspended, and we are joyfully borne up in the air, as it
were in the arms of angels."
—HAVELOCK ELLIS

*N*o one has ever accused me of being much of a sports fan. To reveal the depth of my ignorance, let me begin by confessing a mistake I made some years ago at La Guardia Airport in New York. Standing at the gate for my return flight to Detroit were several men tall enough to scrape their heads on the ceiling of the airport terminal. A friend who was with me exclaimed: "Those guys must be members of the Pistons!" Not to be outdone by her enthusiasm, I rebounded with, "No kidding! The New York Pistons are on our flight!" The Pistons, of course, were my hometown team in Detroit, but I hadn't a clue.

Having thus established my credentials, let me begin by telling you a remarkable story about a man who dreamed of a football team and a winning season. Bill McCartney is former head coach at the University of Colorado and the leader of an international Christian men's movement known as Promise Keepers. Just prior to the 1989 football season, a pastor by the name of James Ryle contacted Bill to tell him about a dream he had about the team.

"The dream foretold that our team, the Colorado Buffaloes, would have a golden season resulting in being ranked number one in the nation and that I, as head coach, would be given the Coach of the Year honors at the season's conclusion. Knowing that James had very little exposure to college football and was hardly versed to be making such predictions, I was personally more than a little dubious. . . . As amazing as it may seem, the dream did come true! After our first game of the season, a victory over the Texas Longhorns, the Denver Post ran a story with the following headline: 'CU Buffs Have Golden Season Debut.' James and I both were stunned to read the words he had seen in a dream actually printed in the newspaper. . . . The season concluded with a rousing victory over Iowa State, followed by a special edition publication titled 'The Golden Season.' Our team was ranked number one, and I was honored with the NCAA Coach of the Year award. . . . That unforgettable season did much to turn my heart toward God with greater sensitivity to hearing His voice. If God would speak in a dream about a football season, what other more pressing matters might He address if we would only listen?"

Whether you are an avid fan or an ignorant bystander like me, you have to admit it was a remarkable dream. Ryle's story caught Bill McCartney's attention, emphasizing the importance of being open to God, however he might speak.

Many of the dreams recounted in Scripture also foretell the future. Think for a moment about Joseph, the younger brother who dreamed he would one day rule over his older brothers. His dream so incensed his ten brothers that they sold him for a slave. "We'll see what becomes of his dreams," they crowed. But years passed and Joseph became a ruler in Egypt. Eventually, he saved his family from famine, moving the entire clan to the land he ruled, thus fulfilling the dream of his boyhood.

The book of Daniel describes a dream of Nebuchadnezzar, king of Babylon, predicting the king would go insane and after seven years be restored to his right mind. It happened just as the dream had predicted.

Gideon overheard an enemy recount a dream to a fellow soldier, predicting that Gideon's army would rout their own. The soldier had dreamed of a round loaf of barley bread that tumbled into camp and struck the tent with such force that it collapsed. After listening to the dream, the second warrior replied, "This can be nothing other than the sword of Gideon. God has given us into his hands." Hearing the dream recounted and its interpretation gave Gideon courage and he and his men won a remarkable victory.

In addition to the stories in Scripture, history is replete with stories of predictive dreams.

The night before he was assassinated, Julius Caesar found himself comforting his wife, Calpurnia, who had suffered a nightmare in which she envisioned a bloodied Caesar dying in her arms. Despite her pleadings that he stay home that day, Caesar went to the senate, where he was brutally assassinated. Calpurnia held him in her arms as he bled to death on the floor of the senate.

Francis of Assisi had a dream while he was yet a young soldier on his way to war. In his dream he saw a magnificent array of shields, spears, and armor. Then he heard a voice saying, "All this shall belong to you and your warriors." At first he mistook the dream for a prediction of distinction in battle. Only later did he recognize it as a prophetic picture of the thousands who would follow his example, becoming spiritual soldiers in the service of the Gospel.

In 1825 John Bosco was nine years old when he had a dream that offered a glimpse of his life work. In his dream he saw a luminous man in a white cloak, who told him he must win boys over with kindness, not the violence he displayed in the first part of his dream. Bosco later founded the Salesians, a religious order of monks who care for homeless children.

In 1865 Abraham Lincoln dreamed of his own assassination. In his dream, he was wandering the White House when he entered the East Room. In front of him were many mourners and a corpse laid out in a coffin, though its face was covered. When Lincoln asked who had died, he was informed: "The president, he was killed by an assassin."

At 3:45 A.M. on June 28, 1914, Bishop Joseph Lany of Grosswardein in Hungary, former tutor to Archduke Franz Ferdinand of Austria, had a chilling dream: "The bishop arose early in the morning from a disturbing dream in which he had gone to his desk to look through some letters. On the top was a black-bordered letter bearing a black seal with the coat of arms of the archduke. The bishop recognized the handwriting as that of the archduke and opened the letter. On the upper part was a light blue picture, somewhat like a postcard, which showed a street and narrow passage. The archduke and his wife were sitting in a motorcar with a general facing them. Another officer was sitting next to the chauffeur. A crowd was assembled in the street. Suddenly, two young men jumped out from the crowd and fired at the archduke and his wife. Accompanying this picture was the following text:

Dear Dr. Lany,

I herewith inform you that today, my wife and I will fall victims to an assassination. We commend ourselves to your pious prayers.

Kindest regards from your
Archduke Franz,
Sarajevo, the 28th of June,
3:45 A.M.

"The bishop jumped out of bed and, with tears streaming from his eyes, noted that the clock read a quarter to four."

Later that day, the archduke and his wife were murdered on the streets of Sarajevo. Their assassination was the spark that ignited World War I.

More recently, George Wallace Jr. stated in the October 11, 1982, issue of *Time* magazine that he had a dream that mirrored the assassination attempt made on his father while stumping for the Democratic presidential nomination in Maryland in 1972. George Jr.'s dream bore an uncanny resemblance to the actual events that unfolded a few days later. The primary difference was that George had dreamed his father had died rather than been wounded by the assassin's attack.

Two ticketed passengers on the *Titanic* dreamed about the disaster prior to the ship leaving port. One heeded the warning of the dream and canceled, while the other perished when the ship went down on its maiden voyage.

My purpose in recounting these stories is not to frighten you nor to encourage the superstitious belief that every dream about the future will come true. It is simply to make the point that such things sometimes do happen.

In fact, there are notorious cases in which the dreamer was misled by a dream. Consider the story of Hannibal, the Carthaginian general who dreamed of a black serpent destroying everything in its path. A young man appeared in the dream, assuring Hannibal that he had been commissioned by the council of the gods to ruin the Roman Empire. Bolstered by the night vision, the general began his laborious invasion of Rome in 218 B.C., even managing to conduct a parade of elephants across the Alps to launch a surprise attack. Though Hannibal won several battles, he was ultimately defeated by Scipio Africanus. Later, he committed suicide rather than face forcible return to Rome.

Or consider the case of Rudolf Hess, the deputy leader of the Nazi Party. In late 1940 an astrologer told Hess that he would be the one who would help achieve peace. Soon after, Professor Karl

Haushofer, a geopolitician admired by Adolf Hitler, dreamed he saw Hess "striding through the tapestried halls of English castles, bringing peace between the two great 'Nordic' nations." Encouraged by the dream, Hess flew to Scotland in 1941, allegedly to pursue personal peace talks with the Duke of Hamilton. He was apprehended and later sentenced to life imprisonment at the Nuremberg trials.

Such stories warn us to proceed with caution before concluding that dreams offer a reliable glimpse into the future. How then should we navigate these difficult waters? James Ryle points out in his book *A Dream Come True:* "One does not discard every twenty-dollar bill given to him simply because a counterfeiter has introduced his forgeries into the market. . . . It is equally foolish to reject genuine dreams and visions in an overreaction to those who use dreams and visions to practice divination and sorcery."

Paul Meier and Robert Wise offer one of the more helpful perspectives on predictive dreams I have encountered: "Obviously the most alluring of all dream forms, predictive dreams are actually quite rare. People often mistake a subjective dream as having a futurist dimension. For example, if we dream of having a car wreck or of our house burning, the warning probably has far more to do with how overextended we are than the possibility of fire or of crashing the car tomorrow. In a great many instances people are not able to identify a predictive dream until the event has passed. *Therefore, we might conclude the purpose of the predictive dream is not to cause us to anticipate the future as much as to recognize the work of God when it comes to pass. . . .*

"Biblical guidelines suggest predictive dreams may appear when some dimension of God's plan is at stake. The content of such dreams puts people into an observant posture, which is important for anticipating what to do as difficult unforeseen circumstances emerge. On the other hand, predictive dreams may give us a road map and encouragement as a new and important work of God unfolds."

In the stories that follow, you will see how dreams can sometimes alter our lives forever, protecting us from harm and reassuring us of God's presence in the midst of difficulty.

"A Dream Brought Us Together"

*J*ack and Rochelle Sutin were both born in Stolpce, a town in eastern Poland. By coincidence, their mothers were the two female dentists in town, though they never knew each other. Shortly after Jack was born, his parents moved to the nearby city of Mir. Both Jack and Rochelle endured unspeakable horrors visited upon the Jews of Poland during World War II. The account of their separate escapes and subsequent love story is told in powerful and vivid detail in their award-winning book, *Jack and Rochelle: A Holocaust Story of Love and Resistance*, published by Graywolf Press. After the war, the Sutins married and emigrated to America, where Jack established a successful import business. Their daughter, Cecilia, graduated from the University of Minnesota, while their son, Larry, earned degrees from the University of Michigan and Harvard Law School. Remarkably, Jack and Rochelle might never have fallen in love nor survived the war had it not been for a dream Jack had in September of 1942.

In June of 1942 we learned that the Nazis were secretly planning to liquidate the Mir ghetto in two months' time. A group of us decided to escape. We fled just four days before the mass killings. Though we had no hope of surviving, we were determined to die in our own way rather than at the hands of those who hated us.

We made our home in the woods, raiding the local farms for food. Living above ground would have been suicide so we carved a bunker out of a small mound of dirt. The entrance was so narrow that only one person could slip through at a time. Once inside, the stench of unwashed bodies fouled the air and made it difficult to breathe. We were like moles packed into a dirty hole. We couldn't help but wonder what would happen when the Germans discovered our hiding place. One grenade lobbed down the entry hole would have blown us to bits. But it was the best we could manage.

Once I got used to the idea that I hadn't long to live, I wasn't afraid anymore. As the leader of the group, I took huge risks, raiding the houses of Nazi sympathizers only two miles from German police headquarters. The police actually put a price on my head, and I was glad to hear it. Jewish life had become much too cheap. Let them pay for a change.

Then, in September of 1942, I had a strange and very powerful dream. I never doubted it foretold the future. My dream gave me a reason to live.

I heard a voice. It was the voice of my mother, Sarah, who had been murdered by the Nazis. She told me I would meet a girl named Rochelle Schleiff in the woods and that she and I would stay together. I didn't see my mother, but only heard her words. As soon as she stopped speaking, I saw Rochelle's face very clearly.

When I woke, I couldn't stop thinking about the dream. Rochelle was an acquaintance of mine before the war, but we had never dated. Why would she appear in my dream? I didn't even know whether she was still alive. Even had she survived the liquidation of the Stolpce ghetto, the odds that we would meet in this portion of the woods were a million to one. It couldn't happen . . . but somehow I knew it would.

I was so sure that I insisted we carve an extra space for Rochelle as we prepared the winter bunker. The others in the group must have thought I was losing my mind, but they went along because they needed me.

Three months later I was sitting in the bunker when one of our lookouts told me that some Jewish women were approaching. When I went out to meet them, I saw Rochelle, standing with two friends. They had heard the story about how this crazy Jack Sutin wanted to save a place in the bunker for a girl he hardly knew.

Rochelle had escaped from Stolpce, where her entire family had been murdered by the Nazis. She and her friend Tanya had narrowly evaded capture and death more than once in their month-long trek in the woods. When I saw her, she was full of lice, wrapped in a blanket, and wearing two left boots. Starving, cold, and dispirited, she had actually been on the point of returning to the ghetto, hoping for a German bullet to end her misery. Fortunately she met a Belorussian farmer who convinced her she was crazy to go back. "Wait! Don't be silly," he told her. "See the little hill over there, near the woods? There are some Jewish boys and girls living there in an underground bunker. They'll help you. Don't go back to Stolpce!" That group of Jews brought Rochelle to me.

Rochelle didn't exactly fall into my arms, but she accepted my offer of shelter. Her friend Tanya was not so lucky. Food and space in the bunkers were at a premium, so I arranged for her to stay with a local farmer who sympathized with us. Later, she was killed by some Russian partisans who raided the farm.

Finding Rochelle was like a miracle to me. It gave me confidence that someone was watching over us in the midst of our hell on earth. I had a new reason to stay alive. For her part, Rochelle was too exhausted to feel much of anything. At first she thought I had made up the dream. But eventually, I convinced her of my love.

What would have happened had I not believed the dream? Only God knows the answer to this question. But I shudder to think how different things could have been had I ignored the message that came to me that night.

A Dream Remembered

*D*ennis and Rita Bennett pioneered a movement of spiritual renewal that swept the nation in the seventies and eighties. Two weeks after their twentieth wedding anniversary, Dennis died, suddenly at their home in Edmonds, Washington. It was All Saints' Day, 1991. Nearly four years earlier, Rita had a dream that seemed to foreshadow Dennis's passing. She recounts it in slightly different form in her book *To Heaven and Back*.

⌇

Dennis was seventy-four when he died. Both of us knew his health was precarious but neither of us suspected that November 1, 1991, would be our last day together on earth.

Ten years earlier, Dennis had resigned as chief pastor of an active Episcopal church in order to devote himself to speaking and writing. That afternoon he was working busily at his computer and I was ensconced in the room next door, glancing up now and then from a stack of paperwork to gaze at the drizzle soaking the autumn trees outside. At 5:45 I headed toward the kitchen to put supper on the table but caught my breath as I passed Dennis's office. I didn't want to believe what I was seeing.

Dennis's chair had fallen backward with his body still in a seated position. His face the color of slate, the look of death was unmistakable.

For years, Dennis had suffered from a heart murmur and a pro-
lapsed heart valve. Not wanting to spend his last days lingering
painfully in the hospital, he had prayed that God would either heal
him or take him home. Mercifully, God had answered that prayer.

But I was left to deal with the aftermath. The husband I had loved
for so long had been taken from me in an instant. For the next two years,
friends prayed with me and talked me through my grief, and I began to
heal from the shock of finding Dennis that day. Several months after
his death I came across an entry in my journal regarding a dream I had
on January 28, 1988, three years and ten months prior to Dennis's death.
Even then, the dream had seemed to foreshadow his passing.

I dreamed Dennis was sitting in a garden and that he was very
tired. He had been washing the leaves of a beautiful plant, covered
with dust. He called me over to look at it. The plant was like no other
I had ever seen. Dennis showed me that the flower at the end of each
branch could be taken off and put back on, like a light bulb being
screwed into a socket. I remember seeing three blossoms for certain,
maybe four, though I couldn't clearly see the last one.

Then I sat on Dennis's lap, laid my hand tenderly on his head,
and began to pray for him. That was all.

Afterward I made the following note in my journal: "Perhaps this
dream means that Dennis has three more years and almost a complete
fourth year." It seemed to me that Dennis was that plant and that each
blossom symbolized a remaining year of life. After that, I simply forgot
about the dream.

Rediscovering the dream after Dennis's death brought tremendous
comfort. God had known the exact circumstances and timing of my
husband's passing. He also knew how shocked I would be at seeing Dennis on the floor of his office that day. I have always believed that God

is the giver of both life and death. But it was heartening to realize he had been preparing me for that difficult moment.

I have little doubt that dreams occasionally speak to us about future events. In this instance, I believe God was speaking through my dream, not to frighten me about the future nor to warn me so I could avoid an impending disaster. Instead, my dream was a gift that helped assure me of God's loving care. Dennis's passing was not an accident in time but part of God's plan for us both. I didn't have to worry whether I should or could have done something to prevent it. Remembering the dream reassured me God was in control of every aspect of our lives.

A Dream of Future Greatness

*Y*ears ago, Pat Lamb Kovic joined the navy, where she met her husband, Tom. After the youngest of their six children started school, she worked as a stringer for two Long Island newspapers. Her second child, Ron, never graduated from college but went on to write a best-selling book, which eventually became a major motion picture, starring Tom Cruise. *Born on the Fourth of July* tells the graphic story of a young man's coming of age in the midst of the hell of the Vietnam War. Oliver Stone, the man the *L. A. Times* dubbed "the most dangerous man in America," directed the film and used his considerable talent to paint Pat in the most unflattering light possible. There was, Pat admits, "some truth to the portrait because to my children I guess I always have seemed very Catholic. When I complained to Oliver, he simply said, 'Someone had to play the villain.'" Remarkably, she bears him no ill will and simply says what matters most is that Ron's story was told—that his life has had an impact on the nation.

🌣

My memory, never strong, has only gotten worse with time. It's hardly surprising, then, that I cannot remember a single dream of any significance except one I had more than thirty-five years ago. It was about my son, Ron.

The scene was of a presidential convention, with red, white, and blue bunting, men wearing straw hats, a podium, a microphone, speeches, and the noise of many voices. I did not know who the front-runner was nor what the issues were, I only knew I was there with my fourteen-year-old son. Suddenly, a man approached and tapped me on the shoulder. He pointed to Ron and said: "Your son will be the man of his generation." That was all. Then I woke up.

I laughed about it when I told my husband, Tom, the next morning. It seemed so preposterous, but that's how dreams are. I didn't remember my dream until years later, when Ronnie was addressing the Democratic National Convention.

Ron was born on the fourth of July 1946 in Massapequa, New York. He was a real firecracker of a boy. A Cub Scout, a Little Leaguer, and a wrestling champ in high school, he couldn't wait for the day he was old enough to enlist in the marines. We were all patriots in those days. He signed on for two tours of duty in Vietnam and wanted more than anything to return a hero to his country. In 1968 his wish came true. My son came home a hero—a twenty-one-year-old who had been hit in the shoulder by sniper fire. He would never walk again. Ron was a paraplegic.

The horror of what had happened to him and thousands of others in that pointless war took a while to sink in. But when it did, he began to speak against the war in Vietnam with a passion that surprised us all. Here's how he describes it in *Born on the Fourth of July*:

> I went totally into speaking out against the war after that. I went into it the same way I'd gone into everything else I've wanted to do in my life—the way I'd gone into pole vaulting or baseball or the marines. But this was something that meant much more than being an athlete or a marine. I

could see that this thing—this body I had trained so hard to be strong and quick, this body I now dragged around with me like an empty corpse—was to mean much more than I had ever realized. Much more than I'd known the night I cried into my pillow in Massapequa because my youth had been desecrated, my physical humanity defiled. I think I honestly believed that if only I could speak out to enough people I could stop the war myself. . . . Yes, let them get a look at me. Let them be reminded of what they'd done when they'd sent my generation off to war. . . . There was no end to what I had to tell them.

And tell them he did. Ron was interviewed on national television when he and other veterans disrupted the 1972 Republican National Convention. Then, in 1976 he was invited to address the Democratic National Convention. Relentlessly, he spoke out—at rallies, in newspapers, on prime time, in a book and a movie that told the story of an American tragedy. My son had indeed become "the man of his generation."

Ron paid a tremendous price to address the nation about a conflict that troubled its soul. But he stood in the midst of his suffering and told the truth as he saw it. I will never believe his agony has been in vain. My prayer for Ron and for our country is that the story of "the man of his generation" will not be forgotten, that it will instead live on, strong enough to shape the hearts and minds of the men of this generation and every generation yet to come.

A Dream of Warning

*D*avid Flaherty lives in Westborough, Massachusetts. He was raised a Christian Scientist but lost interest in religion as a teenager. As he grew older and achieved certain personal goals, he began to feel something was missing. He had put God on a back burner for too long. Maybe it was time to start paying attention to the spiritual side of life. Several years ago he became active in a church, where he currently serves as a eucharistic minister. One night he dreamed of a terrible accident. He walked away from the wreck, but his aunt was thrown from the car. Her body lay motionless in the middle of the road. He wondered whether to warn her.

༝

I dreamed that my wife and I were riding in the backseat of a car in Worcester, Massachusetts, traveling along route 122 A. I remember the exact location, because it passed by a restaurant we frequented once or twice a year. Other than that, we never ventured into that area. My uncle was driving and my aunt was in the passenger seat. All of a sudden, a red pickup cut us off and we were forced to swerve to the right, crashing into a parked car. Auntie flew through the front windshield and was lying on the road in front of the car while emergency technicians performed CPR. I didn't know whether she was dead or alive. The rest of us sustained only minor injuries because we had been wearing seat belts.

The dream was so vivid that I can still picture it. It made me wonder whether my aunt was even ready to die. The rest of our family were people of very deep faith, but I really wasn't sure what she thought about God. She didn't attend church regularly and hardly ever received communion. As a eucharistic minister this really bothered me.

When I told her about the dream, I felt compelled to tell her she needed to make a choice: either she should start wearing her seat belt or she should go back to church. Doing both would be best. She heard me out but seemed a little embarrassed. I did notice, however, that she attended church more frequently in the months that followed.

Fortunately, neither she nor I had much reason to drive anywhere near the location where I dreamed the accident occurred. About a year after the dream, my wife went into the hospital to deliver our youngest child. But there were complications and she was transferred to a different hospital in order to deliver the baby. You guessed it. The new hospital was located close to where I had dreamed the accident occurred.

Soon after the baby was born, my aunt came to visit. On the way home from the hospital, she remembered my dream and buckled her seat belt. Before she knew it, a pickup cut her off and forced her into a telephone pole. An emergency crew had to cut her free from the car with the jaws of life. Though she suffered some injuries, she would certainly have gone through the windshield had she not been wearing her seat belt.

The details of the dream and the real accident varied slightly. Rather than forcing her into a parked car, the truck caused her to crash into a telephone pole. She was with her sister when the accident occurred, rather than with us. The whole thing happened two or three miles from where I had dreamed it had. Still, the accident happened in a town she rarely visited. The essentials were the same.

I'm not superstitious about my dreams. In fact I rarely remember them. But one thing I do know. All dreams are not created equal. I know God gave me this one for a larger purpose. Considering how things turned out, I'm glad I paid attention.

This Dream Came True

*J*ody Lorenzen is a senior in high school, who lives in Colorado with her parents, an older brother, and two younger sisters. Last year she had a dream that may have saved three lives. Like David Flaherty's dream, it warned of a potential tragedy.

৵

My brother, Jonathan, and I were in Monterey, California. We had brought two friends with us for a two-week visit to my grandparents' home. My grandparents were generous with their car, and we had driven it around most of the time we were there. But it bothered me that I was the only one who wore a seat belt. I mentioned it a few times, but nobody paid any attention.

After about a week and a half, I had a dream that we got in a terrible wreck. I don't remember the details, but I do remember the ambulance and the lights and the awful knowledge that I was the only one who survived. It was so horrible. I had to go home by myself and break the news to my family.

I was never so glad to wake up from a dream.

That day we decided to visit an amusement park about an hour away. As we drove, I told everyone about it, but just as before, they seemed to blow it off. On the way back, the two guys started goofing off in the front seat. Suddenly the car swerved and hit the median. We flipped and did a complete rollover. I was stunned but alive. It seemed as though my nightmare had come true. But when I opened my eyes, I realized everyone was fine. The top of the car looked like a pop can that somebody had stepped on. All the windows had shattered. Remarkably, all four of us had been wearing our seat belts. Each one of us walked away from the accident, grateful to be alive.

One of the guys said, "Jody, didn't you just have a dream about us getting in a wreck?" We all started talking at once, amazed that each of us had put our seat belts on when we got back into the car that day.

You might think my dream was a product of anxiety, and maybe I was a bit anxious. But it's hard for me to believe that somebody upstairs didn't have an awful lot to do with it.

Three

❧

Dreams That Guide Us

Life and dreams are leaves of the same book.
—ARTHUR SCHOPENHAUER

few years ago, I was going through a rough period. It was an in-between season, a waiting time in which I both longed for change and dreaded its arrival. For more than sixteen years, I had worked for the same company and lived in the same town. I enjoyed my work, but it had become far too predictable. I didn't want to solve the same problems, jump through the same hoops, achieve the same goals year after year. I needed a fresh challenge. A place to develop new skills, broaden my horizons. The problem was, I didn't know exactly what I was looking for. And I was painfully aware that a new job would mean a new city, new friends, new church, and new home. After sixteen years of heading in one direction, I looked into the future and drew a blank.

One night I woke up with the thought, crystal clear in my head: "You are in the desert right now. You are in the wilderness."

Waking up in the middle of the night may not sound like much of an achievement to you, but it is something I have never been good at. I've slept through tornado warnings and cat fights. I've talked in my sleep and walked in my sleep and never missed a moment's rest. I am a gifted sleeper. But that night I sat straight up in bed, finding comfort in the words that woke me. But why, you may wonder, would words like "desert" and "wilderness" be of any comfort at all?

I had been so anxious and confused about the future that I wondered whether I was even on God's radar screen. The words in my dream assured me God knew exactly where I was, even if I didn't. They helped pinpoint my location on a spiritual map. The desert was a place of testing, the wilderness an opportunity for learning obedience and trust. Jesus, himself, had spent forty days in the desert. Like the children of Israel, I was heading toward a land of promise. I just hoped I wouldn't take forty years to get there.

I don't know why God sometimes makes things so clear at night that seem so muddled during the day. I only know that he can use our dreams to guide us through situations that challenge or frighten us.

Christopher Danz is a freshman in high school who had a dream a couple of years ago that made a strong impression in his life. He had been having the same nightmare for about a month and it really bothered him. Though he doesn't remember many details, he does remember that whenever he focused on an object in his dream, it would become very small and then start spinning counterclockwise, faster and faster and faster. For some reason this terrified him so much that when he woke up, objects in his bedroom would seem to grow smaller and smaller and then begin to spin uncontrollably, just like in the dream. His nightmare repeated itself frequently over the course of a month, until one night it altered its shape.

"I was having the dream, when suddenly a slab of stone appeared right in front of my face so I couldn't see anything else. It looked like it was some kind of marble and had handles on either side and an inscription on it. As soon as I saw it, I grabbed on to the handles. When I looked closer, I realized the inscription read: 'Jesus Is the Rock.' It blocked out all the stuff that had been scaring me, and I never had the dream again."

Christopher was familiar with the scriptural references to Christ as the "rock," or the "cornerstone," so the slab of marble in his dream made perfect sense. Jesus was someone he could hold on to, no matter what was happening in his life.

I had dreamed of a desert and Christopher had dreamed of a stone, both scriptural symbols, rich with meaning. God was communicating his care and guidance to both of us in terms we would understand.

In the fourth century, the Emperor Theodosius revenged the murder of a Roman governor by massacring more than seven thousand people in Thessalonica. After Ambrose, the bishop of Milan and the man responsible for the conversion of St. Augustine, heard the news, he had a dream in which God instructed him to call the emperor to repentance, that he might publicly confess his sin. Ambrose wrote the following to the emperor:

"I have written this, not to confound you, but that by the example of these kings [he had cited examples of several kings who had repented publicly of their sins] may stir you to put away this sin from your kingdom. For you will do it away by humbling your soul before God.

"You are a man, and it has come upon you—conquer it. I urge, I beg, I exhort, I warn—for it is a grief to me that you, who were an example of unusual piety, who were conspicuous for clemency, should not now mourn that so many have perished. Conquer the devil whilst you still possess that wherewith you may conquer."

Ambrose believed the dream had forbidden him to conduct religious services or offer Communion in the presence of the emperor: "I have been warned, not by man, but plainly by Himself that it is forbidden me. For when I was anxious, in the very night in which I was preparing to set out, you appeared to me in a dream to have come into the Church, and I was not permitted to offer the sacrifice. . . . I dare not offer the sacrifice if you intend to be present. Our God gives warnings in many ways, by heavenly signs, by the precepts of the prophets; and by the visions even of sinners."

After several months, the most powerful ruler on earth was brought to his knees, repenting for the thousands he had so callously slain.

Another, more remarkable story of guidance is told about Jacobo Dante, the son of the famous poet Dante Alighieri. Thirteen cantos of

Dante's *Paradiso* were missing after the poet's death, and it was assumed he had never completed the work. A year and a half after his father died, Jacobo dreamed that Dante appeared to him, a radiant look on his face and clothed in white. The poet took his son by the hand and led him to a room in which he had frequently slept. Touching the wall, he simply said, "What you have sought for so much is here."

The next day, Jacobo visited the house where Dante had spent his last days, discovered a wall in his bedroom that was covered by a mat, and found the thirteen cantos tucked safely behind it.

Prior to the Civil War in America, Harriet Tubman, an escaped slave, daringly led hundreds of men and women to freedom in the North by means of the underground railway. Harriet claimed that dreams helped her locate safe passages, preventing her from ever losing a single slave.

Sometimes our dreams may guide us simply by telling us things we already know. Rabbi Jonathan in the Talmud makes this point when he says, "A man is shown in his dreams what he thinks in his heart."

But how can we know and not know something at the same time? Let me cite an example from waking life that was instructive for me. Years ago, a college roommate of mine was taking a musicology course, listening endlessly to South American Indians drumming their drums and chanting their chants. "Doesn't that sound just like one of Simon and Garfunkel's songs?" she remarked after one particularly exotic tune. With a blank look, I assured her it sounded like nothing I had ever heard before. Five minutes later, she caught me whistling the very same Simon and Garfunkel tune she had been thinking of. Sometimes we don't realize how much we really do know. Our dreams may be one way to flush such knowledge to the surface.

Ultimately, dreams are merely one source of guidance among many. And though they can't make our choices for us, they can provide interesting insights along the way.

The dream stories in this section assure us that God works in marvelous ways to keep us from harm and link us together through the power of prayer.

A Dream of Life and Death

*P*aul Grams has been a firefighter for the city of Rockford, Illinois, for fifteen years. Forty-four years old, he and his wife, Val, have a son and two daughters. His remarkable story assures us that the veil between the natural and the supernatural is not always as thick as we might think. Raised in the church, Paul has always believed that miracles can happen. Two years ago he experienced a miracle that saved his life. It unfolded through a dream.

ॐ

Firefighting is a dangerous profession, but that's what I signed up for. Unfortunately, it's harder to be married to a fireman than to be one, at least that's what my wife, Val, says. In fact, she usually has difficulty sleeping whenever I'm on duty. Strangely enough she slept peacefully through the early morning hours of April 3, 1995, when I was fighting for my life.

Ron Hill, John Brazones, and I were veteran firefighters, so I wasn't worried when we were called to the scene of an apartment fire. A neighbor told us he thought an old woman and her grandchild might be trapped in the second-floor apartment. We had no way of knowing that neither of them were at home that night.

The apartment was filled with dense smoke, so thick you couldn't see the beam from your own flashlight unless you held it right in front of your face. As soon as we realized we were alone in the apartment, we knew it was time to get out. Our tanks held 2200 pounds of air pressure and we figured the warning bell might go off any minute, signaling that only 500 pounds remained. Depending on conditions, that meant we would have just three to five minutes left to breathe. But the smoke was so dense we became disoriented. Remarkably, none of us panicked.

Ron radioed the district fire chief and asked that he order the other firefighters to ventilate the building, breaking windows so the smoke would disperse. For some reason, though, the message didn't get through and we were stunned to realize no one understood our danger.

By now we were crawling on the floor, feeling for a way out. A picture flashed through my mind of a photograph I had seen in a firefighter magazine. It showed hand prints in the soot on the wall where a firefighter had vainly searched for a window just a few inches away. He never made it out. Now I wondered if the three of us were about to become the next headline.

Just then I bumped into someone. It happened several times. Each time I asked, "John, is that you?" "Ron, is that you?" No one answered, but I heard a voice in my head saying, "You will never get out of here alive." Despite our danger and the death sentence I had just heard, I felt complete peace. It was as though another voice, one I trusted, was also speaking to me: "Don't worry, people are praying for you. You're going to be all right." I assumed Val was praying, because she often awoke in the middle of the night to pray.

Just then, John's bell went off. We kept groping but couldn't find a window. About three minutes passed and I knew John would soon be in trouble. Actually he had already run out of air and was holding his breath, desperate for a miracle, when his fingers found the glass. He smashed the window with both hands, and we all made it to safety. I was descending the rescue ladder just as the air in my own tank ran out. Due to a malfunction, my warning bell had never sounded.

It was about 1:20 A.M. when we escaped the apartment, but our job wasn't done. The fire had begun in the basement, so we waded around in knee-deep water beneath the building to check for problems. Several of the floor joists had burned through, and we worried the structure would collapse, trapping us beneath the water. Fortunately, we succeeded in safely extinguishing the fire by about 5:00 A.M. At 5:45 I called Val to tell her not to worry. The 6:00 news would carry the story of how the three of us had been lost in the fire and almost died. I wanted to catch her before she saw it.

After it was over, we congratulated ourselves on our good fortune. Each of us knew how close we had come to becoming part of the rubble of that burned-out apartment. Had we panicked, we wouldn't have made it. Our air supply would have been sucked empty long before we found a way out.

That day, my wife left for her job at a local elementary school. Later, she overheard a conversation that startled her. One of her coworkers, Sherry Zahorik, was telling a friend about the "strange night" she had just experienced. Sherry knew nothing about my being in a fire, so Val nearly fell off her chair when she heard the details of Sherry's dream. Here's what Sherry told her:

"I awoke at about 1:00 A.M. with such a heaviness on my chest I could hardly breathe. I felt I was supposed to pray for someone in trouble. As I was praying, a dream unfolded before my eyes. I could see three people in a completely dark room, covered by a very foggy-like smoke. I didn't know who they were, but I could see them frantically searching for something. I felt I was right there with them, watching them go through the whole thing. There was confusion and something worse than confusion—an evil presence that permeated the room. One of them kept bumping into something and calling the names of his friends, thinking it was them. Then this presence would laugh and say, 'You will never get out of here alive.' As I heard that voice, I saw a picture of a man clawing at a wall, trying to reach a window. The wall was full of nail scratching, and blood was running down the window.

"By this time I was out of bed, praying up a storm. Each time I would try to go back to sleep, the heaviness would return so strongly I couldn't breathe. I knew I had to keep praying until whatever it was was over. Finally, about 4:00 or 5:00 A.M., the pressure in my chest lifted and I felt at peace. It seemed to me the crisis had passed. Everything was going to be all right."

Anyone who has never been in a fire couldn't possibly have described it as accurately as Sherry did. The smoke can be so dense and dark that it blots out light and even deadens sound. Val knew enough about my experience to be absolutely bowled over by the story of Sherry's dream. Someone had been praying for me after all, countering a terrible presence in the darkness that was trying to destroy my hope.

I know Sherry was given a vision that night to enable her to pray for us in the midst of a very desperate situation. Thanks to her prayers none of us panicked, depleting our air supply before we could escape the fire. By the grace of God, I am alive to tell the story.

Bird in a Cage

*E*lizabeth Newenhuyse is a writer, speaker, and the author of several books, including *God, I Know You're Here Somewhere: Finding God in the Clutter of Life.* She is also a frequent contributor to *Today's Christian Woman* and lives in Wheaton, Illinois, with her husband, Fritz, and daughter, Amanda.

A lot of people don't pay attention to dreams, but I have always dreamed vividly and often remember them.

When I was small, I would have what I called sky dreams, where the horizon is brushed a fiery pink or the moon a golden orb I could almost clasp in my child's hands. These dreams evoked a sense of beauty and yearning and a longing so palpable it almost scared me. My dreams have always been crammed with color and sound. As a writer, I have wondered whether I am particularly sensitive to such perceptions. At times I have felt God speaking through them, often by way of images that are important to me.

Before I tell you about my dreams, let me say that I love birds. I love to watch birds (and am pretty good at identifying them), I've usually lived with a bird or two, and I have a feeling that birds must be some of God's favorite creatures.

But the bird in my dream wasn't flying or singing. It was clinging to life at the bottom of a cage.

I well remember the dream, which repeated itself over the course of several years. As I dusted the furniture, I would come across a pretty cage. At the bottom would be a small bird, so weak he couldn't hold on to his perch. Suddenly, and with great remorse, I would realize the bird was starving. I had forgotten to feed it. Frantic, I would rush to find some birdseed.

I knew that dreams usually reflect something about the dreamer, so I began to think about mine. What was it saying to me? Why wouldn't it go away? Apparently I wasn't getting the message, and so it kept repeating itself.

As I replayed the dream, I began to think I was the bird in that cage. For several years, I had been living a too-full life. Not full of the kinds of things that nourish your soul, but packed with distractions, busyness, and a stifling kind of clutter. I had been extremely busy with a demanding job and all the responsibilities that belong to the mother of a small child. I felt pressured and weary and began to wonder whether the dream was telling me I was neglecting certain facets of my life.

Finally, after praying and talking with my husband, I decided to quit my job. We would find a way to make do without it. My decision didn't instantly cure what ailed me, but it gave me room and space to breathe. And, interestingly enough, I never had that dream again.

Lately, I've been having another recurring dream, but one I really enjoy. The daughter of an architect, I am fascinated by houses. In my dream I am wandering through a home that seems familiar. I walk from room to room, all of which are rather large. Suddenly I open a door to one I have never seen before. I peer into a pine-paneled family room. Another time it is a woman's bedroom. Each dream is slightly different.

I do not yet understand what the different rooms represent, but I do know that I am that house and that I am exploring the rooms of my soul. It is a bracing and challenging and intriguing adventure. And I am absolutely certain it is a place where I will meet God.

A Dream of Dying

*T*am not prone to prophetic dreams. My dreams have been alternately funny, embarrassing, and troubling. Only once have I had a dream that forced me to my knees to pray for someone who might be facing an impending tragedy. It came to me first in May of 1984. In July, the dream was repeated in slightly different form.

Harold and Luci Shaw were people I admired, though I didn't know them well. Luci had contributed a chapter to a book I had edited, entitled *Bright Legacy: Portraits of Ten Outstanding Christian Women.* She had written about Elizabeth Rooney, a talented but little-known poet. Describing a poet as "little-known" seems a waste of words, since even great poets find it difficult to get into print. But Luci herself is the exception to that rule, a gifted and sensitive writer, who has published numerous books.

Years earlier, she and Harold had founded a small but highly respected publishing firm. They were a couple with an unusually strong marriage, who seemed to share clear-sighted spiritual goals.

In May of 1984 I dreamed that Harold died. I can't recall the specifics, because I didn't pay much attention at the time. I had dreamed of people dying before and nothing sinister had happened. So I shrugged it off—until I had a similar dream two months later.

I was in England, attending a booksellers' convention held every spring in Blackpool, on the banks of the Irish Sea. The perfect setting for an Agatha Christie novel, our Victorian-era hotel was a place universally disliked by publishers, who found it remote, run-down, and anything but convenient for conducting business. But Blackpool in the off-season is a bargain that British booksellers cannot afford to turn down.

In my dream I was walking through a hallway in the hotel where other publishers had gathered during a break in the convention. I still remember the large, reddish flowers squashed to form a printed pattern in the yellow-gold carpet. Small tables covered with linen cloths and loaded with tea and biscuits lined the walls. Here and there a dim light pierced the windows to reflect palely on the men and women who occupied the tables and milled the hallway, catching up on the latest publishing gossip.

"Did you know that Harold Shaw died last week?" asked one of the American publishers. I was shocked. "No, I hadn't heard he was ill," I replied. Then I woke up.

This time, I was troubled. It seemed important that I had dreamed of Harold's death a second time. I felt a strong urge to pray—but not for Harold. For Luci. I asked that she be given strength for whatever lay ahead. And I kept praying through the weeks that followed.

About two months later, in the fall of that year, Elizabeth Rooney, the poet whom Luci had written about, called me with the news that Harold had been diagnosed with lung cancer. The doctors had predicted a life expectancy of less than eighteen months. Would I please pray for him and for Luci? Elizabeth couldn't have known that I had already been praying for two months.

For the next year and a half, I interceded, as did countless others, for this well-loved couple. Harold died in January of 1986.

Three years after losing her mate of thirty-two years, Luci wrote about her experience in her book *God in the Dark.* She begins her story with these poignant remarks:

"I remember. I remember the dark clouds moving across the years of my life, stretched like a field of prairie wheat in the sun, dulled by the sudden shadows. Like the wandering weather, my seasons of doubt and questioning have often come and then moved on.

"Near the beginning of one of my longest, darkest cycles I remember praying with my friend Karen: 'God, show me your self, your reality clear as the sun, no matter what it takes.'

"I didn't know what it would take.

"Another prayer, later, under the same dark clouds: 'Lord, I promise never to give up on you, never to desert the faith.' Like a marriage vow that sometimes staples a faltering relationship, that promise held me during seven years in which I battled to know my God real in the dark while living in his silence, in the sense of his absence."

Her book spoke eloquently and honestly about how faith can grow in the midst of a silent darkness. I hadn't known of Luci's struggles until I saw them spread across the pages of her book.

Once Harold was diagnosed, people all over the world began praying. After his passing, I asked myself why I had been given a head start when I wasn't particularly close to either Harold or Luci. As I have chewed on this question, I have wondered whether my dreams didn't somehow reflect the powerful truth that I am part of what Scripture calls "the body of Christ." I believe God was merely activating one member of the body to do her small part. Consider this passage from 1 Corinthians 12: "God has combined the members of the body . . . so that there should be no division in the body, but that its parts should have equal concern for each other. If one part suffers, every part suffers with it. . . . Now you are the body of Christ, and each one of you is a part of it." I have sometimes been tempted to reduce this passage to a lovely simile: we are *like* a body, living for the same purpose. But, no, the Scripture's meaning is far more shocking and raw: those who believe actually *are* a body. There is a spiritual connection. Our souls are linked. Even our dreams tell us this is so.

"My Dream Prevented Me
from Making a Mistake"

$\mathcal{L}$uci Shaw has remarried since her husband, Harold, died in 1986. A writer, poet, and photographer, she is a gifted woman who knows how to make the most of life. An avid traveler, she has sailed the Great Lakes, crisscrossed the country numerous times with her car and tent, and even gone bungee jumping in New Zealand. Luci teaches at Regent College in Vancouver, Canada, part of the year and makes her home in California. She is the author of many wonderful books, including *Polishing the Petoskey Stone*, *Postcard from the Shore*, and *Writing the River*. Shortly after Harold's death, she had a dream that gave her confidence when she most needed it. A few years later, another dream kept her from making a mistake she may well have regretted the rest of her life.

✣

After Harold died, I felt absolutely overwhelmed, as though treading water in very stormy seas. I would get slapped in the face by a wave and then choke and sputter and nearly go under.

Anyone who has lost a spouse knows that grief is only part of what makes bereavement so painful. Suddenly I was saddled with a bewildering array of legal and financial decisions I had never before handled. In my case, it was worse because I was forced to take the helm of our small publishing firm, which Harold had skillfully directed for so many years.

I felt both saddened and betrayed. How could he have left me alone to face this chaos? He and God seemed to have fled at precisely the same moment. I lived each day, bracing for the next wave, hoping and praying it would not capsize my small boat. One night, when I was feeling particularly low, I had a dream that changed everything:

Harold's warm smile and welcoming voice greeted me as I stepped off the plane. "Glad you're home, honey." It was good to be back, to feel his arm around me as we gathered my luggage and made our way to the parking lot. As soon as we reached the car, Harold handed me the keys and simply said, "You drive." The gesture surprised me, because he usually drove whenever we were together. But I slipped behind the wheel with a sense of relief. Harold sat in the passenger seat next to me. Then I woke up.

It was such a simple dream but tremendously comforting. It felt good to have Harold beside me again. Always an encourager, the Harold in my dreams was acting true to form. Handing me the keys was his way of giving me permission to take charge of new areas of my life. Instead of feeling abandoned, I felt a new assurance that God was with me. Looking back, I now see that my struggles have enabled me to develop stronger spiritual muscles and the skills I needed to live on my own.

Three years later, I had another, more startling dream that prevented me from making a serious mistake. Though Harold and I had had a wonderful life together, I wasn't particularly interested in remarrying. Hard as it had been to lose him, my life had regained a sense of balance. It was both rich and interesting, and I saw no reason to change things. But then I began to date an attractive man who had been a family friend for years.

While Harold had been thirteen years older than I, David (not his real name) was seventeen years younger. An appealing and intriguing person, he and I shared similar interests, and it was always stimulating to be with him. Our conversations were fascinating and far-ranging, and it felt good to have someone care about me again.

Still, I had doubts. I had never pictured myself marrying someone who had been divorced, as David had been. Further, my youngest daughter insisted I was making a huge mistake. At the time, I thought she was overreacting to the possibility I might remarry. But now I know better.

Before long, David invited me to come for a visit. Could I fly out and spend several days with him? He told me he loved being together and that he was serious about our relationship. I felt uncertain and a bit cautious about going. But finally I thought, "Oh well, nothing ventured, nothing gained." Just as I was about to leave on the trip, I had a dream that made me reconsider.

I don't remember much about the dream itself. But I can still hear the voice: "Cancel your plane reservations. Do not make this visit." That was all.

This was an astonishing experience for me, especially since I am always skeptical of people who say God told them to do this or that. Such claims often strike me as simple wish fulfillment rather than genuine spiritual experiences. But I was absolutely convinced that the voice in my dream belonged to God. It seemed a matter of obedience to cancel the trip. So I did.

Not long afterward, I discovered that David had been making similar promises to other women at the same time he was dating me. What would have happened had I ignored the voice in my dream? I have little doubt I would have been inviting trouble. God spoke to me because he loved me.

Now, when I am tempted to doubt his care and protection, I have only to recall the way he encouraged and warned me through these two very different dreams.

A Discerning Dream

$\mathcal{J}$ohn Baker (not his real name) has been active in a ministry of inner healing for many years. People from around the world have benefited from his counseling, prayer, and books. One day, John had a dream that alerted him to a dangerous entanglement involving a staff member and a seriously disturbed woman. Without the dream, John wouldn't have been able to intervene in a way that prevented a young man from getting in over his head.

꒱

My ministry involves counseling and praying with people. To be effective in this kind of work, you need to understand how psychological and spiritual dynamics can impact someone's emotional life. You also need discernment. Though we deal with many people who have garden-variety problems, we also encounter individuals who are deeply and even dangerously disturbed.

For instance, some people repress very deep hatreds. Perhaps they have a secret wish to kill their mother, yet they are quite pleasant on the outside. They may even be people with strong religious commitments who have not yet dealt with the evil in their own hearts. Inevitably, these things fester in the soul and eventually erupt, often by way of pathological transference. Of course psychologists face this all the time. But when it happens to them, they have built-in protections, clinical boundaries that are not available to pastors and others who might encounter such people.

Because I have a very visible position in this ministry, it sometimes happens that certain disturbed people become obsessed with me. I am a father figure whom they idealize—the only one who can help them. They begin to believe I hold the key to relieving their suffering and pain. Understandably, they try to get close to me, to find out where I live, what my phone number is, and so on. But when they discover I am only human and that I don't have a magic answer for their problems, they react in the opposite extreme. All the hate, bitterness, and paranoia that's lodged in their souls erupts and gets redirected toward me or toward others in the ministry. If the person is unstable, it can actually be quite dangerous.

When such people are thwarted, they may try to get close to someone else on the team. When a team member fails to recognize what's going on and begins to sympathize with the person, they begin to do what we call "harboring." They actually provide an environment in which negative behavior can flourish. It's a very unhealthy and unwise response. Unbeknown to me, that's what was happening when I had the following dream.

In my dream I am in the home of a staff member. Richard's house is always immaculate, so I am surprised by what I see. Guests are coming through the front door with various animals in tow. And the animals are urinating all over the floor. I find myself trying to clean up after them. But the more I clean, the more I see many old spots on the floor. It's such a mess that all the rugs are ruined.

As soon as I woke from the dream, I asked God to show me its meaning. Did this person or his house symbolize something about myself, some unpleasant truth I needed to face? As I prayed, I felt certain the answer was no. Later, I called Richard and recounted the dream.

He was so frightened by it that he immediately began telling me about a woman who had been coming to his home who had been deeply disturbed. He had been naïve enough to think he was helping her by allowing her to get close to him. But actually, he had been encouraging her destructive behavior. It was a case of pathological transference that could have had a very bad outcome. As we talked, it became clear that this wasn't the first time this kind of thing had happened.

I believe God gave me that dream so that I would be able to work things out with Richard before the situation came to a head. Though Richard didn't realize it, he was behaving in a way that actually blocked that person's healing. The dream made all the difference.

A House, a Candle,
and a Menacing Darkness

*V*ivian Taylor is a successful salesperson for a Fortune 500 company. A book lover and gourmet cook who enjoys entertaining, she is also the proud owner of one of the sassiest and most charming Scottish terriers I have ever met. Vivian, herself, is an unusually generous woman with a deep prayer life. One night she dreamed of a house, a candle, and a menacing darkness. Normally, a "house" serves as a symbol for the life of the dreamer. But the house in Vivian's dream really belonged to someone else.

&

I love to walk, so it was not surprising to find myself retracing a familiar route in my dream. It was nighttime and I stood for a moment in the street gazing at a colonial-style home with a two-car garage. A candle was burning in the living room. But everything else was black. Actually, I could see a dark cloud surrounding and penetrating the house except for the room where the candle shone.

Then it dawned on me that this was the home of friends. I'd known Tom and Annie for years and enjoyed dropping by to visit them and their three kids. But now there was something terribly oppressive about the scene even though nothing seemed to be happening. I didn't see or hear anyone. Then I woke with a start, feeling really troubled.

I knew someone in that family needed help. The kids had their share of problems, but I hadn't a clue who was in trouble this time. It did seem to me, though, that the oppression I sensed was coming from outside and that it was aimed at a particular person. The lit candle confirmed that God's light reigned inside the house, even though some kind of darkness was assailing it.

I prayed for quite a while that night and in the weeks that followed. One day, I stopped in to see Annie. We were chatting and catching up with each other when she began telling me she had recently been hospitalized with clinical depression. In fact, she was taking medicine to control the depression and was involved in an outpatient program. Fortunately, she was feeling much better.

I decided to tell her about my dream of the previous month. When I finished, she retrieved her journal and started flipping through it. Amazingly, the dream corresponded exactly with her emotional breakdown. Annie felt touched to know that God had been watching over her in ways she didn't even realize. And I felt glad to have been an instrument God used during a very difficult time in her life.

Years ago, I had the sense God was asking me to pray for a harvest I would never see. Sometimes I wake in the middle of the night with the thought that I should pray for someone. It could be anyone—a person I'm close to, an acquaintance, or a public figure I've never met. God just seems to draw back the curtain, showing me what's going on behind the scenes. I may lie awake for two or three hours. Because I don't usually get to see the results of my prayers, I have no way of knowing whether I'm on target. I don't have to know the outcome. I just need to pray.

Though I may never know how most of my prayers are answered, I am grateful God let me in on the secret this one time. My dream was really so simple. It pointed my prayer in the right direction.

Four

⋙

Dreams of Healing

O Lord My God, I cried out to you,
It is you who restore me to health.
You brought me up, O Lord from the dead,
You restored my life as I was going down to the grave.
You have turned my wailing into dancing.
You have put off my sackcloth and clothed me with joy.
　　　　　　—PSALM 30:8–11

*T*f it is possible for dreams to offer glimpses into the future and to guide us in our daily life, might it not also be possible that some dreams hint at the presence of illness before we even experience symptoms?

The idea that our dreams may offer a clue to hidden illnesses dates back to the Greeks. Aristotle, for instance, believed that the "beginnings of diseases and other distempers which are about to visit the body . . . must be more evident in sleeping than in the waking state." Hippocrates, the father of medicine, was a Greek physician from whom we derived medicine's most famous pledge of ethics: the Hippocratic Oath. He believed that dreams could sometimes provide early warning of the presence of disease.

Consider the story of a man who lived in the second century. This man dreamed he saw his father perish in a burning house. Shortly after that, this same man died, suffering a high fever probably caused by pneumonia.

Sometimes a cure rather than a diagnosis is present in a dream. Pliny's Natural History recounts a fascinating incident in the fourth century B.C. involving Alexander the Great and his friend Ptolemaus, who was dying from a poisonous wound. One night Alexander had a dream about a dragon who held in his mouth a certain kind of plant. In his dream, the dragon told Alexander the plant would heal his friend's wound. The plant was obtained and Ptolemaus was healed.

In the seventeenth century, the English architect Sir Christopher Wren faced a rather unpleasant treatment, prescribed to ease the difficulty he experienced whenever he urinated. His physician recommended a bloodletting cure. Before the treatment could be administered, Wren dreamed of a palm tree and a woman handing him some dates. Rather than allowing himself to be bled, Wren immediately procured the dates, which apparently relieved his symptoms.

Another, more recent, and quite different story is told by a woman convinced she was physically incapable of bearing more children. She recounts her dream: "I found myself on a small hospital bed in a strange place. The room was completely white, and I saw nurses in white uniforms. Someone appeared with a child wearing a purple dress. She seemed to be at least one year old and her features were very pretty. A soft voice told me, 'This child will be yours.' I began to groan and beg, 'Take her away. I don't want her.' In that instant, a voice boomed from above me: 'you must have this child.' I cried out, 'No, please. I don't want her, please take her away.'"

After the dream she discovered she was pregnant. Because she had been taking medication that her doctors told her might cause her to hemorrhage and to give birth to a hemophiliac baby, she worried about whether to carry the pregnancy to term. Several times, she nearly scheduled an abortion, but each time she remembered the dream and thought better of it. Eventually, she gave birth to a healthy daughter, whom she describes as "the most perfect angel on earth."

Another pregnancy dream is recounted by Agnes Norton: "Like any other mother-to-be, I worried about whether my child would be healthy. I was anxious about the big things, like spina bifida or cerebral palsy but never about any kind of disfigurement. One night I dreamed I had delivered the baby but that I couldn't see his face. My mother held him in her arms and he was wrapped in a shawl. But she wouldn't let me see the baby's face. Then I woke up. A while later, my son Andrew was born with a cleft palate. At the time I had no idea there had been a history of cleft lips in the family. Fortunately,

Andrew's cleft palate was taken care of years ago through reconstructive surgery and he is fine."

In 1967 a Russian psychiatrist by the name of Vasily Kasatkin published a book entitled *Theory of Dreams*. In it, he summarized his research based on more than ten thousand dreams gathered from twelve hundred subjects. A chapter in his book is devoted to the correspondence between dreams and physical illness. His conclusions shed helpful light on the question of how dreams and illness can interact. Among other things, Kasatkin concluded that illness can increase dream recall. It can also produce distressing images like fire, blood, war, corpses, garbage, doctors, and medicines. Such dreams normally appear before an individual is aware of symptoms, and sometimes reveal both the location and seriousness of the illness.

Citing such research does not imply that all dreams about illness are objectively true. It is certainly possible to dream about an illness when we are perfectly healthy. Nor does it indicate that such dreams always proceed from spiritual sources. But it does point to the fact that we are complex creatures in which physical, spiritual, and emotional factors all work together.

The dreams that follow tell remarkable stories about how dreams have forewarned people of illnesses, sometimes helping the dreamer recover from both emotional and physical afflictions.

A Dream of Angels

*M*arilynn Carlson Webber is coauthor with her husband, William D. Webber, of *A Rustle of Angels*, a book which has sold over a quarter of a million copies. Despite having written about angels, she never laid eyes on one until the summer of 1993. That's when she had a vision of angels—in a distressing dream in the middle of the night.

⌁

I had written an article about angels for *Guideposts* magazine, which resulted in an astonishing flood of mail from all over the world—more than 8,500 letters. You can imagine what my mailman must have thought—perhaps I had invented a cure for cancer or maybe I was selling drugs through the mail.

Hundreds of letters contained such beautiful accounts of angelic visitations that they filled me with wonder and longing. I wanted to see the shining creatures people so movingly described. So one day I asked God to let me see an angel before I died. I didn't know whether he would, but I knew it wouldn't hurt to ask. Then I forgot about my prayer. Several months later, I dreamed of four angels who looked nothing like the magnificent angels I longed to see.

Dressed in long black robes, their faces were downcast and even their wings looked black. They were angels all right, but not the ones I expected. I remember saying in my dream, "Lord, these aren't the right ones. There must be some mistake."

I could tell by the way they carried themselves that they were in mourning. Though I felt intimidated, I summoned the courage to ask one of the angels why they were all so sad. His answer frightened me: "We're sad because you're dying. If something is not done soon, you will die."

When I woke up, I recounted the dream to my husband, Bill. As I was telling him about it, I began to experience pain in my abdomen for the first time. Though I have always been a reluctant patient and hadn't been to a doctor in years, we decided I should call a doctor that day. Before, when I had phoned the Loma Linda Clinic, I was told there was a two-year waiting period for new patients. But that morning Bill got on the phone, insistent that someone examine me.

"Why is it so urgent your wife see a doctor?" the nurse inquired.

Bill knew it sounded crazy but decided to tell her about the dream. She excused herself, saying she needed to put him on hold for a moment. Fully expecting the next voice he heard to belong to a psychiatrist, he was surprised when the nurse returned to say the doctor would see me the following Wednesday.

Tests confirmed I was suffering from ovarian cancer. My doctor had heard about my dream and was amazed I had heeded it. "You have a lot to be thankful for," he told me. "I see so many women who wait too long before seeking treatment. By the time they know something's wrong, it's often too late. Pain isn't a symptom in the early stages of ovarian cancer."

Surgery was set for September 2, 1993, at the Loma Linda University Medical Center. The doctor warned that I was a high-risk patient and would need to be in intensive care for several days after the surgery.

Of course I am a great believer in prayer, so I called friends and asked them to intercede. Expecting to be on edge the morning of the surgery, I was surprised to feel completely at peace. After a few hours in the recovery room, I was wheeled back to my hospital room. I had come through with flying colors. No need for intensive care. No need even for chemotherapy or any other follow-up treatments. The doctors felt confident they had caught the cancer in time.

Why had I experienced pain the morning of the dream when pain isn't a symptom of the disease? Wasn't it to emphasize the message of my dream? I had prayed to see angels of dazzling beauty. Instead, I saw four angels dressed in black. Not the angels I wanted to see, but the angels I needed to see in order to experience God's healing touch.

"A Dream Healed My Fear"

*D*ebby Topliff is the mother of three children. She attended the University of Michigan in the late 1960s and early '70s, when the counterculture was in full swing. Like many students, she was searching for big answers to big questions: Who or what made the universe? If there is a God, does he care about me? What's the meaning of my life? Through a series of misadventures, she eventually discovered deeply satisfying answers to her questions. Throughout the years, her dreams have sometimes yielded surprising insights. She had the following dream on Labor Day 1993.

꙾

I have sometimes wondered whether I might lose my faith if something really terrible happened. That fear must have been lurking in the background when I had a horrible nightmare three years ago, in the early morning hours of Labor Day.

For as long as I can remember I have had a problem with claustrophobia. It especially bothers me if my legs are constricted in any way. The thought that I might not be able to move them is enough to drive me crazy.

In my dream I am trapped in an underground tunnel. I am alone in the darkness, and I can hardly breathe. I have no idea how I got there or what has happened. I only know I am buried alive. I cannot move my legs. I am suffocating. I am so terrified that I wake up.

Afterward, I felt such a sense of panic that I had to get out of bed and walk around, reassuring myself it had not really happened.

Whenever dreams leave such a strong impression, I have found it good to pray about them in case God is trying to tell me something. That morning I asked myself how I would react if I really were buried alive. Would God still be with me? Would I lose my faith? I didn't know the answer.

As I was praying and turning these things over in my mind, it suddenly occurred to me to wonder about the circumstances of my birth. My mother had always told me it had been a breech birth. I assumed that meant I had entered the world bottom first. Perhaps my claustrophobia was connected to this early trauma. As I continued to pray, I felt God reassuring me. Just as he had brought me safely through the birth canal, he would bring me safely through life. Whatever difficulty I faced, he would be there. I didn't think I was imagining the message of his comfort.

Two days later the strangest thing happened. My mother and I were talking on the phone when she brought up the subject of my birth. She had been out walking the dog on Labor Day when a thought popped into her head: "I wonder if Debbie knows about her breech birth." I told her I knew that a breech birth meant the baby came out bottom first. "Not in your case," she told me. "You came out with your legs straight in front of you."

No wonder I was so sensitive whenever my legs felt constricted! It all fell into place. The dream, God's reassurance, my mother's revelation. By praying through the dream and talking to my mother, I had been given a deeper understanding of God's care. I couldn't help but chuckle at God's timing. I knew it was no accident that he began showing me the connection between my fear and the circumstances of my birth on the very day we celebrate as Labor Day.

"The Dream That Saved My Life"

$\mathcal{M}$ary Perretta has seven grandchildren and five children. Of Scottish and Italian heritage, she has always believed in God's care and protection. Though her life has had its share of trials, she has never doubted the words in the book of Isaiah: "The Lord is the everlasting God, the Creator of the ends of the earth. He will not grow tired or weary, and his understanding no one can fathom. He gives strength to the weary and increases the power of the weak." Until now, only her family and a close friend have ever heard the story of the dream that saved her life.

☙

Many years ago, when I was twelve years old, my grandmother Maria died. Our family was close, and we were all so sorry to lose her. Her last days were spent in a local hospital.

Before she died, I had begun to experience stomach pain and nausea. The family doctor prescribed cold packs, but they did no good. Because my mother believed laxatives cured every stomach ailment, I avoided telling her how awful I felt.

About a week after my grandmother's death, I began to suffer severe pain, nausea, and fever. One evening I had a dream like none I had ever had before or since. I saw a tall person whose face I couldn't quite make out. I was told that in two weeks' time I would become very ill and that I must leave the house, refusing any food, drink, or medication, and head for St. Mary's Hospital, ten blocks away.

For some reason, the dream didn't frighten me. I only knew I needed to follow its instructions to the letter. To this day I don't know who the figure in the dream was. Perhaps it was my grandmother, but I can't say for sure.

Two weeks to the day of my dream, I became very ill. Without telling my mother where I was going, I headed for St. Mary's. I had to walk slowly since I was in so much pain. As soon as I entered the hospital I told the emergency room physician that I was ill, my white count was very high, and that I would die within twenty-four hours. I have no idea how I knew this. The words just came out.

One of the nurses overheard me and laughed, saying that I was obviously looking for attention. But the doctor drew some blood, and, sure enough, the tests indicated that my white blood count was dangerously high. The nurse called my home and my father arrived and heard the news that I needed an emergency appendectomy. I remember being carried to a car and rushed to the hospital where our family physician practiced. I was operated on within the hour and awoke in the very same room in which my beloved Grandmother Maria had passed away a few weeks earlier. God had taken one member of our family but through a dream had spared the life of another.

Healed, Body and Soul

*D*avid Hazard is a writer and publishing consultant. The author of numerous books, he is also the editor of *Rekindling the Inner Fire*, a devotional series drawn from the spiritual classics. A reflective man, he is the kind of person whose conversation is so engaging and thought-provoking that an hour luncheon passes easily and pleasantly, as though it were a mere ten minutes. The father of three, he and his wife, MaryLynne, live near Washington, D. C.

⁓

For twelve years I had the same dream over and over, at least three or four times a year. It began when my first child, Aaron, was about fourteen months—just old enough to toddle unsteadily across a ship's deck. Actually, the only ship he has ever been on in his life is the one in my recurring dream.

I was enjoying the breeze as I stood near the prow, gazing across clear Caribbean waters. It was a beautiful cruise ship, floating serenely on smooth waters. As I glanced back across the ship's deck, I noticed Aaron emerging from a doorway near the stern. He began to wobble toward me just as a billowing darkness banished every trace of blue from the sky. Suddenly the ocean began to swirl and heave, forming a huge black whirlpool with the cruise ship perched precariously at its edge. The stern began to tip and I ran frantically toward Aaron, trying to grab him as he stumbled toward me. Just as I was about to scoop him into my arms, he slid backward and fell through the railings into the dark water. I watched in horror as he was sucked to the bottom of the ocean.

I woke terrified, in a sweat, the blood pounding through my neck and temples. Relief came when I realized it had only been a nightmare.

But relief eluded me as the dream repeated itself again and again. My terror escalated with each repetition. When my second son, Joel, was old enough to walk, he took Aaron's place in the dream. As before, the sea swallowed my child, and I stood by, helpless and horrified.

When my youngest, Sarah, began to walk, the nightmare changed, but the effects on me were identical—a sense of looming panic, the knowledge that something terrible was about to happen, my inability to save her.

This time, I dreamed I was in bed but awake. I heard an intruder enter the house and listened as footsteps entered my daughter's room. Everything in me wanted to bound out of bed and rush to her room. But I was a statue, frozen in place, alive to the anguish of my helplessness. I could hear Sarah crying and someone racing out of the house. Once again, I awoke in a sweat.

The last time it happened, the dream was so vivid I actually got out of bed, went into Sarah's room and held her in my arms. I needed to know she was safe. That it had only been a very bad dream.

Finally the dreams stopped but I began to have panic attacks in the middle of the night—especially when I was away from home, traveling on business. It was so severe I actually had to call a friend from Europe in the middle of the night. The chronic anxiety that shaped my dreams had muscled its way into my waking life. This happened two or three times.

In the summer of 1994, within the space of a month, I suddenly had something very concrete to worry about. Through a series of circumstances, I lost half my income, Joel was suffering from what the doctors thought might be a brain tumor, and I was threatened with a lawsuit. We had sold our home, preparing to move out-of-state to take on more consulting work—and then the company decided it could not add me for at least a year. To make matters worse, I had been suffering from chronic fatigue for a number of years and had been diagnosed with rheumatoid arthritis. Stress intensified the disease, and many nights my joints were on fire and my hands would claw out until I soaked them in hot water, working them back and forth in hopes of rubbing the pain away.

Our ordeal lasted for about a year. Though we were living a family's worst nightmare, we managed to survive it pretty well. During that time, we averted the lawsuit, I found work, and we discovered that Joel's health crisis wasn't a crisis after all. In the process, we realized we were more resourceful than we ever thought possible.

One night I woke up with a voice inside my head saying, "Now you understand what that anxiety was all about." I can't really explain it, but I became aware that fear had been stitched into my skin at a very early age because of stressful home circumstances, forming a part of who I was. Constant anxiety had contributed to my chronic fatigue and the rheumatoid arthritis, to say nothing of my nightmares. As I pondered the words, I envisioned a time line of my life. I saw myself as a small boy who had experienced abuse at the hands of a family friend. When I had tried to tell my parents about it, they were speechless— probably too shocked and overwhelmed to do anything. The net effect was that they did nothing to counsel, comfort, or protect me.

Consequently, even as an adult, as a father, I came to live with the constant, vague sense that something terrible, something outside my control was going to happen. I could do nothing to stop it. No wonder I had that recurring dream about my children—my precious ones whom I wanted to cherish and protect. The nightmare was confronting me with my most deeply rooted fears.

That night, God helped me put my finger on what had been bothering me for so long. It was as though he were saying, "You have carried this fear all your life, thinking you would not have the strength or resourcefulness to deal with the crises that came your way. But you have just lived through one of the worst years many people can imagine. And you survived. I helped you through it—giving you the strength and know-how to handle every crisis. I was in control of your circumstances the whole time. I let you experience the crisis in order to heal your anxiety and show you that no matter what happens, I will take care of you."

It was as though a sliver of fear had been jammed into my soul. To get it out, God used his big thumbs to squeeze me. Not a pleasant experience, but one vital to my healing.

Even before the crisis hit, I had another dream that helped me cling to God and trust him in the midst of all my health problems. My struggles with chronic fatigue and arthritis had convinced me I couldn't find security in the usual places: in my health, strength, or career. God was teaching me to be strong in spirit even though weakness characterized every other aspect of my life. One night I had a dream—at least it started as a dream.

I dreamed I was awake in bed, surrounded by a shaft of white light. I was saturated with this penetrating light, which came through the ceiling. By contrast, everything else was pitch black.

At some point I opened my eyes. I was no longer dreaming. Though I couldn't see the light, I felt overwhelmed, as though I were lying in a sort of lightfall—like a waterfall made of light and love. It was such a great feeling that it took me a few minutes to realize I was in absolutely no pain. Even the knuckles of my toes felt fine. My hands were normal. I was at peace.

A passage from Scripture came to mind: "Keep yourself in the love of God." Keeping myself in the love of God meant trusting him more than I trusted myself. It meant surrendering my physical well-being to him. It meant refusing to believe evil of him even though I didn't understand why he was allowing me to suffer. If I kept myself in his love, I would remain in this lightfall.

When I told MaryLynne about it, she wondered if I had been healed. But I didn't really care. I just wanted to keep myself under that lightfall, to stand under God's outpoured love.

By the next night the pain had returned. It remained with me for some months, in fact. But eventually, it disappeared completely, and I am now living a normal life. My doctors say I am in remission. Whether it is a remission or a complete healing, I believe I began to get better once the spiritual and emotional components of my illness had been dealt with. The fear, the doubt. I didn't get one of those miraculous moment-in-time healings. Instead, my healing was a process involving a profound change in spirit, attitude, and life-focus—also changes in diet and lifestyle. Through it all, God has been shaping my soul for a purpose, not just to heal me but, in part, so that I can be useful to others who are facing their own struggles and difficulties.

A terrifying dream and a dream of great beauty—two very different experiences brought healing to my soul and to my body.

Five

❧

Dreams of Wisdom

I've dreamed in my life dreams that have stayed with me ever after and changed my ideas; they've gone through me like wine through water, and altered the color of my mind.
—Cathy Earnshaw
in Emily Brontë's novel Wuthering Heights

Who doesn't remember the dream of King Solomon, said to be the wisest king the world has ever known? Young Solomon had inherited the throne of Israel from his father, David. One night, after worshiping God, Solomon was given a dream that transformed his life.

In the dream, God appeared and told him to ask for whatever he wanted. With surprising humility, especially for a king, Solomon replied: "I am only a little child and do not know how to carry out my duties. Your servant is here among the people you have chosen, a great people, too numerous to count or number. So give your servant a discerning heart to govern your people and to distinguish between right and wrong."

Pleased that Solomon hadn't asked for long life, riches, nor the death of his enemies, God responded: "I will do what you have asked. I will give you a wise and discerning heart, so that there will never have been anyone like you, nor will there ever be."

Blessed was the man who recognized the value of wisdom and knew it to be a gift of an all-wise God.

In the thirteenth century, Thomas Aquinas, the most brilliant man of the times, had a dream that helped him complete a difficult theological passage over which he had been laboring with no result. One morning, he entered the scriptorium and began dictating the passage to his *Summa* as though he had known the answer all his life. When the surprised scribe asked how he had so smoothly and easily resolved the issue, Thomas replied that a dream had instructed him and given him the key to understanding the theological issue in question.

George Frideric Handel heard the last movements of his masterpiece, *Messiah*, in a dream. Dmitri Mendeleyev, a professor of chemistry in St. Petersburg, dreamed the structure of what became the Periodic Table of Elements. Friedrich A. von Kekule, another chemistry professor, understood that the molecular structure of benzene was ring-shaped as a result of dreaming of a snake biting its tale. Goethe, Charlotte Brontë, Christina Rossetti, Graham Greene, Reynolds Price, William Styron, Katherine Mansfield, and Robert Penn Warren are just a few well-known writers whose dreams have given birth to poems, dramatic scenes, characters, and plots.

Albert Einstein had a dream in his adolescence to which he traced his understanding of the theory of relativity. In the dream he was riding a sled which kept going faster and faster until it approached the speed of light. The stars began to take on fantastic new patterns and colors, dazzling the boy on the sled. Einstein commented that his entire career could be seen as an extended meditation on that dream.

In the June 27, 1964, edition of the *San Francisco Chronicle*, champion golfer Jack Nicklaus sheepishly admitted that a dream had helped pull him out of a bad slump. It had given him the clue he needed to correct a problem with his swing.

Surely if dreams can inspire great music, science, literature, and even an improved golf swing, they can occasionally offer help in resolving personal dilemmas for which wisdom is the only remedy.

To uncover the wisdom hidden in a dream, remember that dreams often have narrative structures, a beginning, middle, and end. When you wake from a particularly significant dream, try to catch the gist of the overall story. Look especially at the way the dream begins since that sets the stage for the remainder of the action. Like a good narrative, a dream will usually present a problem and then try to resolve it.

Note the setting of the dream, the characters, the time frame. What kinds of emotions do various characters in the dream display?

How do they behave? How did you feel after you woke up? Were you excited, sad, astonished, puzzled, amused?

If you take time to think about your dreams, you will discover they are not usually as crazy as they seem. As Pedro Meseguer pointed out in his book *The Secret of Dreams*, "Saying that we can be guided by dreams does not mean by their lack of reason or opposition to reason, but by their reasonableness, which is often greater than one thinks, though it may not be clear at first sight."

As he has also rightly pointed out, the fault of our age has been to overstress the rational elements of life. "To go to the other extreme of overstressing the irrational elements would of course have far more dangerous consequences; the ideal is an ordered and balanced synthesis of all the elements that should go to make up the human personality."

Increasingly we live in a time when people are starved for the spiritual side of life. As never before, we hear of angels, dreams, visions, apparitions, and miracles of one kind or another. Many of us are no longer in danger of scorning the supernatural. Rather, we are in danger of embracing every claim to supernatural experience that confronts us without discerning the source. We welcome whatever appears mysterious or "spiritual" without exercising appropriate caution. In the end, such a reaction can only lead to superstition and spiritual confusion.

But the best defense against superstition does not involve retreating into the old rationalism, safely cut off from realities we cannot see, feel, hear, smell, or touch. Rather, our safety comes from being in relationship with God, allowing Scripture to anchor us, understanding the teachings of our faith, and being open to the leading of the Spirit of God wherever and however we encounter his presence. The God of all wisdom will not fail to help us if we ask.

The dreams that follow did not unlock the secrets of the universe nor inspire the dreamer to pen a poem or paint a great work of art. But they did provide wisdom and discernment for how to handle difficult circumstances.

Falling off Cliffs

*L*auren Andersen is a successful editor with one of New York's largest publishers. She has worked for many years as an acquiring editor with several best-sellers to her credit. Recently, she turned her attention to spearheading and running a very successful book club. Despite her many achievements, she hasn't always been able to appreciate them. Somehow, her successes have been diminished by the feeling that she was never quite doing enough. Here's how her dreams revealed the crux of the problem, enabling her to make some important changes, ones that have helped reshape her understanding of God and his care.

ॐ

Mothers often get a bad rap in our society. They get blamed for everything that's wrong with us, from thumb-sucking to psychotic breakdowns, so the last thing I want to do is add more fuel to that particular fire.

Still, I have to admit that my own relationship with my mother hasn't always been very healthy. Let me start by explaining that she has many wonderful and endearing qualities. She is a woman whose own deep faith has influenced me profoundly. But she is also a woman with an iron will and impossibly high standards, whose two daughters will never measure up to her dreams for them.

I had been raised to think that my sister and I were somehow responsible for her happiness. For instance, my mother never had a driver's license until she was forced to get one after my father's death. As soon as we were old enough, we drove her everywhere. Also, my mother never made plans of her own but relied on my sister and me to entertain her on weekends, even after we grew up and moved to our own homes.

Partly because my mother was a very religious woman I had a hard time separating my idea of God from my relationship with her. As far as I was concerned, they were like two peas in a pod. If I couldn't please her, I couldn't possibly please God.

I'll never forget the time I landed my first writing assignment. A major magazine called and asked me to write a piece for them. Thrilled and certain Mother would share my excitement, I phoned with the news. But her response was underwhelming. "Well, what's the circulation?" she asked. When I told her it was a couple hundred thousand, she only said: "But isn't it a bit flaky?" I assured her it was a respected and influential publication, but she wasn't about to be persuaded. "Send me the draft when you finish it," was all she said.

I hung up the phone, thinking: "I may satisfy other people in my life, one day I may even satisfy God, but I will never ever satisfy my own mother."

Looking back on my childhood, I realize that I was sheltered, dependent, and much too perceptive for my own good. When I was only seven, I began having a recurring nightmare.

Like most children, I had scary dreams about being chased. An enormous lion would come after me when I was playing outside. I would run as fast as my small legs would carry me, certain that powerful jaws would shred me to pieces. But just as the beast was about to overtake me, I would awaken, relieved that I had only been suffering my too-familiar dream.

One night the dream changed and the lion chased me through the yard and right into the house. I rushed to the safest place I could think of—my parents' bedroom. But when I reached it, the door wouldn't budge. My mother was inside, and despite my pleading, she refused to unlock it. She was sorry, she explained, but she just couldn't let me in. As I peered through the keyhole, I could see her on the other side of the door with her arms around two little girls, about my size. But they didn't look like children. They looked like miniature replicas of my mother. She wouldn't open the door because the lion might rush through and attack them. In my dream, it seemed as though the girls were her daughters, sisters I had never met.

Years later, I recounted the dream to a therapist, who suggested that the two girls in my dream represented the two daughters my mother would have liked to have had, rather than the two she did have. She wanted children who would grow up to become just like her rather than two unruly little girls who would one day become women in their own right. That understanding cleared up a lot of the confusion I was experiencing and helped me deal with the tremendous guilt I felt at not being the daughter my mother wanted.

A few years ago, my mother and I both had strikingly similar dreams only two days apart. How such a thing can happen is a mystery to me. But I do know that her dream and mine startled me into a deeper realization that I needed to make changes in our relationship. I was asleep in my old room while visiting my mother at Christmas when I had the following nightmare.

I was standing on top of a tall building in New York City. Though I wasn't in any danger of falling, I was holding tightly to someone who was slipping over the edge. I knew that if I didn't manage to pull that person up, they would fall several stories to the sidewalk below. But as much as I strained and tugged, I just couldn't haul them to safety. Then I realized the person I was trying to hold on to was my mother. But it was no use. I had to let go. As she slipped from my grasp, I woke up. My heart was pounding so hard I was shaking. I was so upset by the dream that I told no one about it.

Two days later, after I had returned to New York, my mother called and said, "Lauren, I've had a very upsetting dream and I just had to call to make sure you were all right. I dreamed you were a little girl and that you had just returned from playing at a friend's house. We were standing outside in the yard and you were telling me that you had obeyed me and that you hadn't gone near a certain street I had forbidden you to cross. And as you were telling me this, you suddenly stepped back and walked straight off a cliff and there was nothing I could do to save you."

My mother was reassured to hear I was well, but I was astonished by the similarity of our dreams. I had tried but failed to save her from falling off the edge of a tall building. She had tried but failed to keep me from walking off the edge of a cliff.

Though our bond as mother and daughter wasn't a healthy one, I believe it was so strong that we somehow managed a deeper kind of communication. Both of us must have been picking up subtle cues that became expressed in our dreams. The dreams convinced me I needed to change the way I related to her. It was time for me to let go of her expectations, to pull back and stop playing the game according to her rules. In a manner of speaking, I needed to walk off the edge of the cliff so that I could start living my own life. I needed to let go of her hand and trust that she would find a way to stand on her own two feet.

Practically, it meant that I needed to establish some healthy boundaries, boundaries that should have been in place years ago. For instance, I decided I could no longer tell my mother about all the exciting and important details of my life. If I did, she would simply deflate them and I would be crushed. Sad as it was, I could no longer afford this kind of intimacy.

I also decided to join an Episcopal Church, a decision that didn't meet with my Baptist mother's approval. As I made these and other changes in my life, it began to dawn on me that perhaps God really did love me after all. He cherished the person I actually was rather than the person I was trying so desperately to become.

Obviously, my difficulties with my mother have a strong psychological basis. But working through these issues has changed my relationship with God. My spiritual journey is no longer based on the need to please my mother, but on a real hunger for God, who I now believe has a unique purpose for my life.

Dreams don't make you a better person. It's what you do with them that counts. But I'm grateful that some of my dreams have given me the insight I needed to become a stronger person and, in the long run, maybe even a better daughter.

"A Dream Helped Save My Marriage"

*L*ois Furdeck is a registered nurse who holds a teaching position in a psychiatric hospital in Yankton, South Dakota. The mother of three grown daughters, she carries photos of her six grandchildren wherever she goes. Currently enrolled in a spiritual direction program, she hopes to help others make progress in their spiritual lives. Seven years ago, she had what she calls a "big dream," an experience that helped turn her life around.

᠉

After twenty-five years of marriage, my husband, Bob, and I were finally alone again. The last of our three girls had just left for college. It could have been a romantic moment, with soft music and nostalgic words whispered to each other as we celebrated all we had achieved in our life together. But neither Bob nor I was feeling particularly romantic. In fact, we wondered if we still felt anything at all for each other.

It had been easy to ignore our problems when we were focused on the kids. Both of us worked different shifts, he as a police sergeant and I as a nurse in a psychiatric hospital. But now our youngest was gone and we had just sold our home and moved to a secluded cabin on a nearby lake. Bob had resigned his position and was searching for a new job so it was no longer easy to ignore each other. Fighting soon became our preferred method of communicating. I was so depressed that the words of an old Peggy Lee song kept droning on and on in my head: "Is that all there is? Is that all there is?" I couldn't help replaying the lyrics, which seemed a hopeless commentary on the state of our marriage.

Fortunately, neither Bob nor I are quitters, especially when it comes to marriage. Once I figured out that we needed to get reacquainted, I felt sure I could handle the problem. I had always been good at fixing things at home or at work so I didn't see why I couldn't figure out a solution to our problems this time. I dragged Bob to every kind of renewal program within a hundred miles. We were going to learn how to communicate if it killed us. But nothing seemed to help. I was on a treadmill, moving faster and faster in my search for a solution but going nowhere at all. That's when I had the dream I will never forget. It happened on January 5, 1990.

In my dream I am standing on a stage all by myself. Huge puzzle pieces are scattered across the platform. Though I am tired, bedraggled, and sweaty, I reach out and pick up the pieces, trying to make them fit together. I do my best to hold them in place as I pick up yet another shape, trying to see where it fits. I hold the puzzle up before an audience, showing them that I can put it together. But it keeps falling apart. And I am falling apart too, crying but determined to fit the puzzle back together. Then I watch it fall to pieces again.

Suddenly I hear a voice, asking: "Why are you trying to do this by yourself?"

The next thing I know I am standing in the bathroom staring in the mirror, not sure if I am asleep or awake. Why am I trying to do this by myself, I wonder. And I shake the sleep from my head. But I cannot shake the dream from my heart.

This is the first dream I have had in years—or at least the first dream I have remembered. Without understanding it, I know it is a big dream and that it represents some kind of turning point in my life.

Later that week, I decided to share it with members of a self-help group I belonged to. Afterward, a woman named Ellen asked if she could talk with me about my dream. "Do you know who that was talking to you in your dream?" I told her I hadn't the slightest idea. "It was God," she said. "He's communicating with you in this dream."

A nominal Christian at the time, I was astonished to think God might be trying to catch my attention through the dream. But Ellen's words rang true, and it was the beginning of a spiritual awakening in my life.

Since that dream, Bob and I have come full circle. Both of us know God in a deeply personal way, and we have experienced him graciously renewing our marriage. Our relationship wasn't transformed overnight. It takes a lot of work and commitment. But the dream marked the beginning of a new era in our life together. It suggested that I end my solitary efforts and begin a new partnership with God.

Like any good nurse, I still struggle with wanting to "fix" things, but I know the best way to solve any kind of problem is to surrender it and follow God's lead.

Bob and I spent six years in our cabin on the lake getting to know each other once again, working through our difficulties and renewing our commitment as a couple. If you had told me then that a dream would mark the turning point in my life, I wouldn't have believed you. But now I realize that God is involved in our lives, whether we're awake or asleep. It doesn't really matter to him.

Jesus in Dreadlocks

*L*ucy Scholand holds a degree in math from the University of Michigan, sometimes referred to as "the Harvard of the Midwest." Her interests include home schooling, languages, swimming, and saving money, an understandable pursuit for the mother of four growing children. In fact, one of her penny-pinching ideas was included in Amy Dacyczyn's best-selling book, *The Tightwad Gazette.* A few years back a television program in Detroit did a feature story about Lucy and her family's money-stretching lifestyle. The dream that follows won't save you any money, but it may cause you to be a little bit more generous when others disagree with you.

꒳

My husband, Paul, and I had been part of a Christian community for many years. Barely out of my teens when I joined, it had been a positive and rewarding experience for the most part. But then something happened that upset me greatly. More than twenty years after its founding, the community began to split apart because leaders couldn't agree on various issues. I felt anxious and confused, wishing the conflict would evaporate. But it only got worse. I felt ashamed of how we were behaving toward each other, convinced that we had let God down big time.

Unfortunately, people I respected landed in opposite camps, and some seemed very certain God was on their side. In the middle of the conflict, the leaders asked us to vote on a particular direction to take in light of our difficulties. I felt confused about what was really going on and unsure of how to cast my vote. I knew I couldn't simply decide on the basis of other people's opinions.

Frankly, I had gotten lazy in my spiritual life. Instead of actively praying for wisdom, trying to perceive what God might be saying to me on a regular basis, I had come to rely more and more on the group's sense of what God was doing. And now the group was headed in several different directions at once. My confusion was running rampant when I fell asleep one Sunday afternoon after church.

I was standing in the kitchen with my daughter. Catherine was five years old at the time, but in my dream she was a baby in arms. She looked at me and spoke in a voice that wasn't hers: "You are distressed, but you don't need to be, because I am coming soon."

Suddenly, we were outside with hundreds of others, waiting excitedly for a parade to pass by. A flatbed truck came rolling down the street and Jesus was sitting on it. But it wasn't Jesus as I have ever imagined him. This Jesus wore dreadlocks. He was a black man dressed in pure white. He invited me to come up and sit down next to him, and I can remember the tremendous sense of peace I felt just being in his presence. Then I woke up.

When I recounted the dream to my husband, Paul, I told him that all the controversy, the disagreement, and the turmoil we had experienced as a group of Christians wasn't really very important. What was important was whether we were living for God and open to his presence regardless of how he might reveal himself.

I think it was unusual for a white woman to dream that Jesus was an African-American who wore his hair in dreadlocks. But that picture helped me see Jesus in all kinds of people. I felt God was warning me against developing religious prejudices, against confining him to a box or acting as if I knew exactly what he was doing in every situation. It gave me a tremendous sense of freedom to simply trust that God was with me.

My infant daughter had spoken prophetically in my dream, saying that Jesus was coming. I have no doubt that he came to me that day and that he gave me a new perspective on our difficulties. When I closed my eyes for a nap, I was confused and restless. When I opened them, I was at peace. Really, it was just that simple.

A Comforting Dream

*H*endrika Vande Kemp is professor of psychology at the Graduate School of Psychology at Fuller Theological Seminary in Pasadena, California. The editor of a book entitled *Family Therapy: Christian Perspectives*, she has recently contributed a chapter to a new book, entitled *Psychology and the Cross*, a history of the School of Psychology at Fuller. Over the course of her career, she has studied hundreds of dreams from a variety of sources. Dismayed by the tendency of neuropsychologists to reduce dreaming merely to a physiological process, she recounts a dream she had in 1985 that had a profound impact on her self-understanding and her spiritual life.

୬

I was born in the Netherlands, the eighth of ten children. I realize now that my mother was absolutely overwhelmed by her large family. I can still picture her, trying to juggle things, nursing an infant at her breast, cleaning up after her two-year-old has wet the bed, then rushing off to comfort the four-year-old who is throwing up in the bathroom. Before she knows it, it's time to feed the baby again. I can see the tears running down her ruddy cheeks—a good mother, who loves her children, stretched taut by too many demands.

An intuitive child, I did not always know how to interpret what I sensed others were feeling. In my own infant way, I concluded my mother didn't love me and that it would have been better had I not been born.

My family moved to the United States and became active in the Christian Reformed Church when I was still a young child. If you know anything about the Reformed tradition, you understand that it represents a highly rationalistic approach to Christianity. In many ways, my home life and religious training were greatly at variance with my personality, which was intuitive, sensitive, and introverted. Painful as it was, these influences probably helped temper me in a good way.

Even so the combination made me feel terribly alone and isolated. I sensed things about people and situations to which others were oblivious. Voicing my perceptions only made things worse, either eliciting puzzled responses or bringing difficult subjects into the open before anyone was ready to discuss them. I had yet to learn that the gift of discernment works best with a good sense of timing.

This feeling of being different and alone followed me into my professional life. I remember how surprised I was when a senior member of the faculty told me I was too impulsive. His comment didn't mesh with the compulsive, orderly side of my personality. I confided in a close friend, who assured me that "impulsive" wasn't on my personality roster. Later, I realized my intuitive style of decision making might look impulsive to people whose approach was highly rational. They couldn't follow my thought process, so it looked as though I were making decisions on the spur of the moment. Furthermore, after taking some personality assessments, I realized that my personality really was rather unusual, which helped to explain my sense of isolation. It wasn't that I was any better or worse than others, I was just different.

I tell you these things so that you can understand why the dream I am about to recount had such an impact on me.

I had studied dreams and Jungian psychology for many years, so I was delighted to welcome Morton Kelsey to Fuller, where he was scheduled to lecture on psychology and religion. Kelsey had written several books on the spiritual significance of dreams, as well as the process of discernment, and he was such a warm and caring person it was a blessing to be with him. In many ways, he seemed a kindred spirit, at least in terms of his personality, which was also intuitive and introverted. He was someone I could relate to and someone who seemed to understand me.

After one of Kelsey's lectures, I had a dream that was a great encouragement to me.

In my dream I see a child sitting on the lap of an adult. At some point, I think that I am that child. Both the adult and the child are facing in the same direction. And together we are paging through a coloring book with drawings of animals and forest scenes. What is on the page isn't important. But what is important is that none of the pages have yet been colored in. The child looks at the coloring book and exclaims with delight, "You mean I don't have to go in by myself!"

I would have expected her to say, "You mean I can color all the pictures!" but she doesn't.

In my dream it seems as though the uncolored pages represent the future. They would be colored in as the future unfolded. The child of my dream is saying to the adult, "You mean I don't have to do this alone?"

Afterward, I realized that Morton Kelsey, author of *Companions on the Inner Way*, had given me some hope for eventually finding a spiritual director, someone whose wisdom and friendship could help deepen my life in God. I wouldn't be alone as I tried to figure things out. Somehow, I felt God had given me this dream to assure me I would have spiritual companions on my journey.

For a child who sometimes felt bereft of the guidance of a parent, and who often felt out of kilter with the rest of the world, this was a wonderful promise and one I have never forgotten.

High Anxiety

*T*had the following dream at the end of October, 1995, just after
I completed work on a book I was writing. I had spent a week's
"vacation" working on the manuscript in order to meet my deadline.
Now it was time to return to my day job as a book editor. As I lay my
head on the pillow that Sunday evening, I made the mistake of rehears-
ing the week ahead. All my anxieties about work came flooding in.

One of my authors had completely changed the outline for his
book. The work we planned to publish had vanished and a substan-
tially different kind of book had taken its place. Unfortunately, he was
determined to strike a new course regardless of what his publisher
thought. A second book was to have been produced on a rush sched-
ule. Thus far, the author hadn't supplied his collaborator with even a
page of material from which to work. Despite promises to the contrary,
countless phone calls, pleadings, and cajolings, we still had nothing,
and the book would undoubtedly be late. These concerns were racing
around my head as I tried to sleep. I shut my eyes and prayed, admit-
ting that I didn't know what to do and asking God's help. The dream
that followed was anything but restful, but I believe it was an answer to
prayer.

$\backsim$

I dreamed I was standing in a hotel room, talking with a friend. Ruth told me she needed to cancel a speaking engagement scheduled for later that day. Would I mind taking her place and addressing a women's luncheon at a local church? I assured her I would be glad to cover for her, but as soon as I said yes, I panicked. It dawned on me that it was already 11:00 A.M. and that the luncheon was scheduled to begin at noon. I hadn't the slightest idea what I would say to the two hundred women who would attend.

"Call a cab. I need to call a cab," was all I could think. But as soon as I turned to use the phone, I discovered that another friend was already using it. Despite sign language indicating I desperately needed the phone, she continued to talk about trivial details to someone on the other end of the line. I was furious at her insensitivity.

By the time I finally made it to the luncheon, all I could think was that I needed to find a quiet room in which to gather my thoughts. I had twenty minutes to decide what I was going to say. Someone pointed me in a direction, and I took off running, hoping to sequester myself until the event began. I soon found myself sprinting across the top of a piano. As I glanced down, I noticed a piece of sheet music resting on the piano, entitled "Be Still and Know That I Am God." Suddenly, it dawned on me—I had been given the text of my talk!

As soon as I reached the room, I began frantically working out the meaning of this verse from the psalms. What exactly did it mean to "be still"? I had been anxious and angry and anything but still. And what about the "God" part? Had I been playing "God" by trying to handle everything on my own? Trying to make sure everything worked out smoothly? In my dream, the insights were coming so rapidly that I tried writing them down so I wouldn't forget them. But, as with the rest of the dream, my efforts were frustrated. I couldn't find anything to write on. Finally I managed to round up a few odd scraps of paper, but every time I jotted a note, I would lose the piece of paper it was written on. As the luncheon was about to begin, I woke up.

When I opened my eyes, I realized that the message "Be Still and Know That I Am God" was meant for me, not for the women in my dream. God was trying to get through to me about my own anxiety. I was running too fast, doing too much, trying to take charge of things that were outside my control. I needed to stop saying yes to the impossible demands I placed on myself, to slow down and learn to be still, letting God be God in every situation in my life.

I was intrigued by the piano and the sheet music in my dream and wondered what they might represent. A few days later, I happened across a note in a book by Paul Meier and Robert Wise, entitled *Windows of the Soul: A Look at Dreams and Their Meaning*. At the back of the book is a section containing a list of various dream symbols and their possible meanings. Here's what it said about music: "Music is a source of peace and well-being. The symbol may suggest inner harmony and could signal things are going well." In fact, things were definitely not going well. Still, I couldn't help but wonder whether God wasn't speaking to me about the inner harmony I lacked and longed for. Wasn't he telling me that internal peace came, not from striving to do everything perfectly, not from saying yes to every good idea, but from quieting my soul in his presence and letting him reveal himself in the midst of my circumstances?

As so often happens, the books I was worried about when I went to bed that night turned out just fine. Looking back, I have to wonder how much energy I regularly waste by not surrendering my anxieties to God in the first place. My dream hasn't "fixed" the problem. But it has caused me to reexamine my priorities, to ask myself whether I am running ahead of God or responding to his initiative. Who knows? If I can learn the lesson my dream is trying to teach me, I may not need to learn it the way I usually do—the hard way, through painful experience.

Six

❧

Good-bye Dreams

We sometimes congratulate ourselves at the moment of waking from a troubled dream: it may be so at the moment after death.

—NATHANIEL HAWTHORNE

*W*hen I began seeking stories to include in this book, I had no idea I would hear from so many people who had dreams of loved ones who had died, often quite suddenly. Always, these were vivid dreams. The dreamer was grappling with some kind of trouble prior to the dream: a father's spiritual condition, a too-vivid memory of death, the inability to say good-bye. There was unfinished business. Fear, depression, confusion, grief— these were the emotions that filled the dreamer before the dream. Wonder, peace, joy, assurance—these were often the aftereffects of what I have called good-bye dreams.

There was one exception, where the dream so startled a man that it sent him into a severe insulin reaction.

In addition to dreaming of those who had already died, some people shared stories of dreams that predicted a death. Though the dreams may have frightened them at first, later they seemed a source of comfort. God had planned to take their loved one and he had softened the blow by announcing it in advance.

Did these people actually meet their dead in dreams or did it only seem so? Many of them describe the experience as being absolutely real, stronger than any dream they have ever had. It is interesting to note that St. Augustine didn't believe the dead actually appeared in dreams. Instead, he thought it likely that such dreams were messages from God delivered by angels.

Certainly Scripture is clear in condemning the practice of consulting the dead, linking it to witchcraft. Fortunately, that is not what is being suggested by these dreams. None of the people who had them were attempting to conjure up their loved ones. And none are insisting that their dead actually appeared to them. Instead, their dreams came unbidden, bringing messages of peace and assurance.

Since our dreams make use of symbols, uniquely meaningful to us, it is hardly surprising we would dream of those who have died. What symbol could be stronger than the picture of someone we have loved? Augustine's explanation makes sense to me: God uses such dreams to send us messages.

Of course there are many cases throughout history of such dreams, particularly those in which the dreamer foresees his own or another's death.

Polycarp was the bishop of Smyrna (in modern Turkey) who was martyred in his eighty-sixth year. Three days before his arrest, in the second century A.D., he dreamed his pillow was set on fire. After that he told his companions he would be burned alive. Eyewitness accounts describe the scene of his martyrdom as he was bound to a stake and set afire: "The fire, shaping itself into the form of an arch, like the sail of a ship when filled with the wind, encompassed as by a circle the body of the martyr. And he appeared within not like flesh which is burnt, but as bread that is baked, or as gold and silver glowing in a furnace."

In the year 203, Vibia Perpetua, twenty-two years old and the mother of an infant son, was imprisoned because she refused to renounce her faith. One night she dreamed of a bronze ladder extending to heaven. On the ladder were swords, lances, hooks, and other instruments of torture. Beneath the ladder, she saw an enormous serpent who tried to terrify anyone who would ascend the ladder. She saw a fellow martyr ascend first. Once he reached the top of the ladder, he called out to Perpetua, urging her to beware of the serpent but to climb up the ladder after him. In her dream, Perpetua climbed to the top, where she saw an immense garden.

Despite the pleading of her father to save herself for the sake of her infant son, Perpetua suffered peacefully a violent martyrdom, refusing to renounce her faith.

St. Augustine tells the story of a young man by the name of Gennadius who was having doubts about whether there was an afterlife. In Gennadius's dream, he was shown a beautiful city. The next night, a young man appeared in his dream and said to him: "After your death, while your bodily eyes shall be wholly inactive, there shall be in you a life by which you shall still live, and a faculty of perception by which you shall still perceive. Beware, therefore, after this of harboring doubts as to whether the life of man shall continue after death." Augustine concludes the story by commenting that Gennadius learned about the reality of the afterlife through his dream.

In more recent times, after his capture during the American Civil War, the explorer Henry Stanley dreamed in considerable detail about the death of his aunt four thousand miles away in Wales.

When you hear such stories, you might well wonder why such predictive dreams are not more common. Certainly these are extraordinary accounts. Perhaps the most that can be said is that God is the only one who knows whether such a dream might serve a good purpose.

Before and after a death, dreams can heal our grief. In her book *God in the Dark*, Luci Shaw recounts the dream of her friend Georgia after the death of Luci's husband, Harold. "Georgia tells me she dreamed that she and Bernie were dining at our house and after helping me in the kitchen she entered the dining room to see Harold sitting at the head of the table. 'Luci thinks she's all alone,' he told her, 'but I'm watching, and I know everything she does.' Another message from God through my friends, and an absolutely supernatural answer to my prayer for Harold to know how much I miss him."

Our good-bye dreams link this world to the world beyond, giving us hope that we may one day be reunited with those we love. They call attention to our need for healing, convincing us it is time to put an end to sorrow as we begin to resolve our grief.

The stories that follow speak about the way dreams can bring comfort and healing in the loss of someone close to us. They can also alert us to the need to pray for others.

A Dream about Mom

Charlene Ann Baumbich (pronounced "Bombeck," but no relation to the famous Erma) is a born communicator. "I occasionally have brilliant thoughts," she admits with a big grin, "and love passing them on—whether they concern the good, the bad or the dubious." Her articles have appeared in numerous publications, including the *Chicago Tribune*, the *Chicago Sun Times*, and *Marriage Partnership* magazine. She is the author of *Don't Miss Your Kids*, *How to Eat Humble Pie and Not Get Indigestion*, *Mama Said There'd Be Days Like This (But She Never Said How Many)*, and *The Twelve Dazes of Christmas*. She and her husband, George, are currently surviving midlife together in Glen Ellyn, Illinois. In 1975, she got a phone call that her mother had suffered a massive stroke. Two weeks later, her mother was dead. Here is the story of a powerful dream that healed Charlene's memory of her mother's last days.

جم

My mother had been named after a racehorse. Though I never met the horse, I always knew this mother of mine was a champion in her own right—beautiful, graceful, fast-paced, and vibrant. As far as I know, Nellie Ruth hadn't an enemy in the world, even though she once emptied a punch bowl over the head of a blonde bombshell who was putting the moves on my dad. When she was nine months pregnant, she drove a delivery truck to help my father's new business stay afloat. Both feminine and fearless, she could shoot skeet or skin a rabbit with the best of them. Once she even shot a fox that made its way into the basement of our farmhouse. She had energy, passion, and guts. A person of unstoppable spunk, she was beautiful both inside and out.

Mom never went anywhere without her toenails painted, her hair done, and perfume trailing. Never, until the night of January 14, 1975. She was only fifty-six years old when she suffered a massive stroke. I got the call in the middle of the night and flew to Albuquerque the next morning, fearing the worst.

My fear exploded the moment I walked into her hospital room. Surely that body lying on the bed couldn't belong to my mother! All the life, the beauty, the laughter had fled. There was only a limp figure, hooked to a machine, with tubes protruding from every orifice. It was more than I could bear.

For the next ten days I stayed with Mom, combing her hair, misting her body with cologne, clasping her hand, desperately hoping to restore some semblance of the woman I had known and loved. I tried not to cry in her presence, unsure whether she could sense my tears. Her neurologist pressured us to pull the plug, but we just couldn't. We had hardly adjusted to the idea of her illness when he told us that her condition was hopeless: "It's as though someone extracted your mother's brains, scrambled them, and stuffed them back into her head. They're useless," he explained in the most brutal bedside manner you can imagine. We didn't know whether Mother would die or whether she would live another thirty years in that horrible condition.

In the midst of this, I met an angel named Dorothy Booker. To pass the time, I had been working on a macramé project, when this wonderful, round, black woman, whose mother was also in the hospital, started talking to me. Before I knew it, I began pouring out my grief and pain. So many decisions needed to be made about Mom's care. I didn't know what to do. I had never lived through a crisis without drawing strength from her, and now she *was* my crisis. Mom was the one who always told me how beautiful I was. She lavished praise on my cleverness. She admired every hokey crochet project as though it were the most exquisite work of art. She was the foundation I stood on, the ground that steadied me. If she wasn't there to tell me these things, who would be? What would I do without her bountiful laughter?

Dorothy Booker enfolded me in her comforting bosom as I sobbed out my grief. "Child, the Lord has your mamma right here in the palm of his hand. No matter what you decide, he knows what's best for your mamma. He loves your mamma more than you can imagine, and he is in charge of your mamma." Dorothy eased my grief and comforted me like the angel she was.

After ten days, I returned to my family in the Midwest. Sadly, my last vision of my mother was a tragic one. Colorless, an oxygen mask covered her mouth, and she lay with one eye open and the other closed. What a horrible last impression of my smiling, joyous, large-hearted mother! The memory haunted me.

Four days later I got the news that Mom had died. Somehow I made it through the funeral, though I was falling apart inside. Weeks followed in which I found myself irritated at anyone who crossed my path. I couldn't understand how friends and family had suddenly grown so stupid! No matter what they did, they drove me to distraction. I began to realize I was the one with the problem.

Then I had a dream more vivid and real than any I have ever experienced.

I saw my mother standing in a glass telephone booth filled with light. The background was smoky gray and misty, somewhat ethereal. But a bright light surrounded my mother. I couldn't talk to her or touch her, and she didn't talk to me. But we communicated. Her face was absolutely at peace, and she was smiling at me with a brilliance I had never seen before. I can only say she looked beatific. Healed, whole, and utterly happy. It was as though she were saying, "Charlene, I'm well and you are going to be all right. You need to know this."

I woke up weeping but completely at peace. It was an absolute gift of God. The dream had diminished the ugly memories of my mother's illness and replaced them with the most beautiful vision of her I have ever seen. Dorothy Booker's words came back to me. "Child, the Lord has your mamma right here in the palm of his hand." My mother was well, and so was I in that moment.

So many people are burdened by tragic memories of a loved one's death. I hope the story of my dream will help diminish such memories for others, so that they will not remember their dead in a way that utterly contradicts who they were in life. Despite my mother's suffering, I know she is more beautiful than ever. When I close my eyes, I can see her laughing up a storm, enjoying herself as never before. Knowing she is well and with God gives me joy.

A Dream about Dad

*C*onnie Neal is an inspirational speaker with several books to her credit. A former businesswoman and youth minister, she lives with her husband, Patrick, and their three children in Antelope, California. The youngest of seven children (five of them half-siblings), she was shuttled back and forth each week between two sets of parents: her mom and her husband, Abie, and her dad and his wife, Edith. The story of her remarkable childhood is told in her book *Dancing in the Arms of God*. Her father died when she was twenty-six, just three weeks after she had given birth to her first child. The circumstances of his death disturbed her deeply, but she found surprising peace through a dream she had several days after his funeral.

꒜

My father was a tornado of a man. Eccentric and driven, he was brilliant in his own way. He was a compulsive gambler with an explosive temper and more creative ideas than were good for him—or anyone in his orbit.

At one time, he had more than twenty different business cards with his name on them, remnants of small enterprises he had started and then abandoned. He generated enough quick bursts of energy to short-circuit a mainframe computer.

We lived in a three-bedroom house in a nice little neighborhood right across from my junior high school. Ours was the corner lot, with a large lawn in front and a big backyard. Dad would start projects in the garage, which would spill onto the patio, which would ooze into the backyard, which would creep to the top of the six-foot fence. When the yard was completely crammed, with only a two-foot path to walk on, he built ten-foot extensions on the walls.

Some of his projects did rather well until the gambling took its toll. It was frustrating to watch his repeat performances: a grandiose idea followed by a grandiose effort, soon forsaken for the next grandiose idea. Over the years, his losses mounted.

Dad was going to make something of himself if it killed him. By the time he was in his early sixties, he had cashed in his life insurance policies, sold everything he could get his hands on, and taken out a second mortgage on the house. Eventually, he and my stepmother, Edith, lost their home and ended up moving in with my sister and her husband.

Looking back, I realize my dad may have suffered from what would now be diagnosed as Attention Deficit Disorder. He couldn't seem to control the compulsive thought patterns and behaviors that drove him. Despite his shortcomings, I always knew he loved my sister and me, and I was grateful he had somehow managed to provide for us, his only children. As I grew older, I prayed God would reveal his love for him and that Dad would have the grace to slow down. A few years before he died, he became a Christian, though he rarely attended church and I didn't see much change in his behavior.

I will never forget the last great idea Dad had before he died. He was seventy years old. It was 1984 and I had just given birth to my first child. "Honey," Dad said. "I need you to make some flyers for me. I'm starting a new business remodeling bathrooms." I knew better than to point out the folly of his latest moneymaking scheme. "Make it clear on the flyer I'm offering a ten-year guarantee," he insisted. The irony of a seventy-year-old guaranteeing his workmanship for ten years was completely lost to him. He wasn't trying to deceive anyone. He was determined to work hard and fast and wasn't ready to take leave of the planet until he had finally achieved something.

In December of 1984 I spent the evening with him in my sister's home. Uncharacteristically, Dad seemed tired and went to bed early. In the middle of the night, he suffered a severe heart attack.

"Get my pills," he screamed to Edith and my sister. They hadn't even known of his heart problem and hadn't a clue where the pills might be. He clutched his chest and yelled at Edith to bring him the newspaper. Flipping frantically though the paper, he pointed to an ad: it offered cremation for only $400. My dad spent the last moments of his life worrying about money for his own funeral. It was heartbreaking. The day before I had been typing up the flyer with the ten-year guarantee. Now my father was dead.

We managed to give Dad a decent burial after all. But I was terribly disturbed by his passing. He had always had such grand aspirations for himself and his children. It was frustrating to watch him fail so often, because he had instilled in me the confidence that I could do whatever I set my mind to. His philosophy had worked for me, but failed him, and troubled me.

I never minded that Dad wasn't able to leave me with any kind of material inheritance. I didn't need or want that from him. But I wondered if there was any other legacy I could draw from his life, any lesson I could glean. The night after the funeral, I prayed, asking for wisdom in the midst of so many disturbing feelings. That's when I had the dream.

I dreamed I was back in our old house, after the funeral. Just like old times, I looked for Edith and asked if I could climb in bed with her, something I had done as a child whenever I felt afraid or alone. "Come on, Kiddo, you can get in bed with me," she replied. "I don't want to be alone either." We both dozed off and then heard the front door open and close. Someone was whistling and clambering around, knocking into things in the living room.

Edith and I looked at each other, but neither of us were afraid. We knew who had entered the house. The bedroom door banged open and there stood my dad. He was beaming, standing tall, dressed in a new pair of khaki work pants and a crisp flannel shirt. Around his waist was a brand new utility belt, loaded with shiny tools. "Dad, what are you doing here?" I said.

A grin spread across his face and he said, "Well, I had to show you people. I had to come and tell you that I finally found a place where I am appreciated." He was laughing when he said it. "They know what I'm worth up there."

"But Dad, don't you know you're dead?"

"Of course I know I'm dead," he replied, still chuckling. "You see these tools? The Lord gave me these, and I'm up there working on the mansions right now. Well, that's all I wanted to say. I finally found a place where they know what I'm worth." Then he left without saying good-bye. He turned around, whistled, and was gone.

It was just like my dad to barge in and then leave without a proper farewell. When I woke up, I couldn't help but think that his lifelong dream had finally been realized: he had at last found acceptance and real appreciation. He was cherished as he never had been on earth.

I know my father was a man with many problems. But I also know that God is merciful. After my dream I couldn't stop thinking about the passage in Scripture that says: "For no one can lay any foundation other than the one already laid, which is Jesus Christ. If any man builds on this foundation using gold, silver, costly stones, wood, hay or straw, his work will be shown for what it is, because the Day will bring it to light. It will be revealed with fire, and the fire will test the quality of each man's work."

I was acutely aware of my father's failings. If it had been up to human beings to pass judgment, most of us would have said, "Boy, is he going to get a talking to when he gets there." And maybe he did get a talking to. I don't know. But the Scripture is clear: in the process of entering into God's presence, the Lord lets the fire sweep away everything that isn't of him, and all that's left is good. God sees the true kernel of the man. He knows that some of the people who seem weakest might be better than we are because of what they've struggled with. Each of us has a path to walk, and God is the only one who knows how well we've managed it.

Did my dad really appear to me or did I simply dream about him as a way of resolving intolerable tensions? You may wonder. I don't fully understand how such things work, but I do believe the dream was more than my psyche playing tricks on me. Whatever the case, I am certain it was a gracious answer to a heartfelt prayer.

A Christmas Dream

*E*ileen Kindig is a contributing editor for *Marriage Partnership* magazine and the author of *Good-bye Prince Charming: The Journey Back from Disenchantment*. A former newspaper reporter, she describes herself as an avid reader, an antique collector, and a pretty good cook. In November of 1987 she had a dream about her sister-in-law, Carol, who had passed away a year earlier.

Carol and I were linked by marriage but never by friendship—at least not in the early years of our relationship. But to my surprise, we actually started to like each other after she had her first heart attack. She was only forty years old at the time, and the experience affected her profoundly. Never a religious person, she suddenly became interested in spiritual questions and eventually developed a very deep faith. Unfortunately, she made the characteristic mistake of new converts by pressing her convictions on unsuspecting friends and family members. Before long, I was the only one who would listen, and we grew close as a result.

When Carol was only forty-five she died of a massive heart attack. Though I was grateful for our five years of friendship, I hated losing her. She left behind a husband who seemed lost without her and a twelve-year-old daughter.

None of us expected that Dan would ever remarry. He was such a stay-at-home kind of guy, we thought it unlikely he would meet anyone. But he surprised us all by falling in love with an old high school acquaintance. They planned to marry within a year of Carol's death.

The whole family was delighted for Dan, but others in his circle disapproved. They thought he was jumping the gun, so soon after Carol's death. I'm sure Dan felt the pressure of their disapproval. Just before the wedding I had a dream about Carol, so strange and so wonderful that it really didn't seem like a dream.

It was Christmas Eve and Carol and I were in the kitchen of her log-cabin home, cooking up a storm. Suddenly, we heard a knock on the back door. Though we had been standing side by side when I went to answer the knock, I was surprised to see Carol on the other side of the door when I opened it. She was wearing a long Mary-Poppins-like coat.

"Come out and close the door and don't let anyone know I'm here," she whispered. She took hold of my arm as I stepped outside into the soft hush of a snow-covered world, my nose filling with the freshness of pine trees standing pencil-straight in the chill air. "Come, let me show you something," she said. All of a sudden she opened an umbrella and we went soaring through the starry expanse of sky, just like Mary Poppins. I felt as though I were flying through a van Gogh painting.

As we floated over forests and homes and the white world below, she said, "See what's here." I looked down and felt an incredible sense of peace. Though she didn't say it, Carol seemed to be sharing her perspective on everything that was happening down below. She was telling me she was happy and at peace and that she was glad Dan was planning to remarry.

To describe the experience sounds like nothing, but to have done it—I actually felt I had done it—was incredible. To this day, nine years later, I can envision every tree. I can see the moon wedged into a sky full of stars. I can see Carol and the expression on her face. The wonder of that dream took my breath away.

About a week later I had another, less vivid, dream in which Carol actually said she thought it was wonderful Dan was remarrying.

What was I supposed to make of my Christmas Eve dream? Despite the Mary Poppins motif, I knew it was profoundly spiritual, unlike anything I had ever experienced. But I didn't know whether to tell Dan about it. I decided to say nothing, at least for the time being.

Four years later, my husband and I were sharing Christmas dinner with Dan and his wife when the conversation created a natural opening to speak of the dream. I hadn't planned to. It just happened. "I'm so glad you told me," Dan said. "I've never dreamed about Carol since she died, but it's wonderful to hear your story."

Should I have told Dan about the dream before his marriage or should I have waited? Even now I don't know the answer to that question. Whatever the case, I am certain that Christmas Eve dream became a Christmas gift to all of us that day. It spoke about a life beyond this world, about the happiness and safety of someone we had loved and lost, and about the longing we all have to know there is more to life than we sometimes realize.

Dreaming of Mentors

*S*haron Rogers holds an M.A. in Christian education from United Theological Seminary. A newspaper columnist, author, and mother of two school-age children, she describes herself as a homemaker, a writer, and a juggler-in-training. In the last few years, she has had dreams which forewarned her of the deaths of two important women in her life.

∼

I can still feel soft pink cheeks rubbing silk-like against my own as Grandma gathered me into her arms and held me tight. No matter what I did, no matter what happened, I knew those loving arms were as firm and real as mountains surrounding a city. No child, I believed, could ever be in danger with such love encircling her.

But now the mountains were trembling. Those strong arms had become weak with age and illness. And I was away at college, wishing I were home beside her.

One day, during a break between classes, I began to feel uncomfortable and irritable, as though life were slightly out of kilter. I headed to my room hoping for a catnap to ease the tension. I slept for about ten minutes and had a simple dream.

Nothing much happened. I saw a clock, whose hands moved slightly as I watched. Then I said to myself, "It is over, and peace is restored."

I woke up, grateful that my frustration had disappeared. Later that day I visited an elderly woman from our church, who wasn't well enough to leave home. As I read from the scriptures to comfort her, I had the strange feeling my grandmother was nearby: "Count it pure joy, my brothers, whenever you face trials of many kinds, because you know that the testing of your faith develops perseverance. Perseverance must finish its work so that you may be mature and complete, not lacking anything."

As soon as I returned to my dorm room, I received a message to call home. In that instant, I knew I would never feel those loving arms around me again this side of heaven. Sure enough, my grandmother had died that very day.

The clock in my dream had symbolized the moment of her passing. The words of the Bible, "Consider it pure joy," had been meant for me as well as for the elderly friend I had visited earlier that day.

Hard as it was to lose someone so dear, I felt at peace. This woman who had loved me so lavishly, was now cradled in the arms of God, himself. I knew she was well.

Sometime later I had another dream, on St. Patrick's Day of 1994. It concerned Colleen O'Brien, a person more proud of her Irish blood than anyone I had ever met.

A woman of fierce loyalties and strong habits, she was a nurse who knew better than to smoke but did anyway. Whenever she ran out of cigarettes, she simply borrowed a few of her husband's small cigars. A capable woman, who loved her husband and her children, she was like a mother to me. I had known Colleen was ill but hadn't an inkling of how serious her condition was until my St. Patrick's Day dream.

In my dream, I walked into a house that was more like a day-care center than a normal home. Children were everywhere. Active and noisy, they were obviously well cared for. Just as when my grandmother had died, I felt a sense of discomfort, but this time it was in a dream.

I moved from room to room trying without success to find a quiet, comfortable place in the midst of the chaos. Then I saw Colleen O'Brien. Dressed in a pastel blue skirt and a white Victorian high-neck blouse, her hair was tucked into a lovely twist. A soft white glow surrounded her. I couldn't see her face, but we recognized each other. She was calm and serene, the exact opposite of everyone else in that house.

I watched in silence for a moment as she finished a small sewing project she held on her lap. Mesmerized by her calm, I was aware of the contrast with my own anxiety.

"So why are we here?" I asked.

"You must say good-bye to me."

I was floored because I knew exactly what she meant. This woman I esteemed so highly was about to die. I felt frustrated, saddened, and lost.

"But wait . . . ," I started to say. "Look at all these noisy children, and the house is so cluttered."

Colleen simply replied, "There's really nothing here worth worrying over. Think about what they represent [the children]. Think about what this means. I am well, and I am at peace."

But I didn't know what she meant. Then my best friend, Janet, walked up beside me and said, "Cheryl, you've missed the point here. You're too literal. Come with me."

So we left the noisy house and walked through a gorgeous green field, as peaceful as the house had been chaotic. My frustration vanished and the dream ended.

Later that day I learned just how ill Colleen was. Not long afterward, I attended her funeral.

Colleen O'Brien has been gone for a while now, but I still remember her as she appeared in my dream—the soft white glow, the high-necked and long-sleeved blouse, hair folded neatly behind her head. She was the image of feminine wisdom, peace, and tradition.

As I have thought about the dream, I realize that Colleen, like my mother and my grandmother, was a woman who showed me what it means to hold in my hands the deep responsibilities of home, husband, children, work, and community. In my dream, the house symbolized my own anxieties as the mother of two young children and as a woman who at times feels overwhelmed by her roles as writer, homemaker, and juggler par excellence. I was searching for the peace and tranquillity that Colleen had already achieved.

Since then, I have come to realize that I don't have to figure out how to handle everything entirely on my own. I am linked to women of past generations who have successfully navigated this territory before me. Though smoking cigarettes and an occasional cigar will never be part of my repertoire, I hope I can learn to live the wisdom of Colleen O'Brien well enough to pass it on to my daughter's generation. Perhaps some day my face will glow with an inner serenity and I will be able to echo Colleen's words: "There's really nothing here worth worrying over."

A Dream in Time

*C*raig Galik grew up in West Mifflin, Pennsylvania. A dyed-in-the-wool baseball fan, he played in the semipros until he was thirty-nine and then sponsored a team called the West Mifflin Rebs. He owns a tavern, which he named after another of his teams, Rounding Third. He and his wife have two children. In 1987 he had a dream about his father that encouraged him to talk openly about the things that really matter.

When I was thirty, my folks finally divorced. My father's drinking and womanizing had become too much for my mother to bear. He was an alcoholic who owned his own bar. Eventually his drinking cost him everything: his wife, his children, his home, and his livelihood. I didn't understand how a man could be so irresponsible. For years he had failed to pay the bills because he spent his money on liquor and women. He was nobody's idea of a good father, and I resented him for it.

As I got older and became more serious about my faith, I tried to do what little I could to help others. One day it hit me. Every month I was sending a few dollars to India, to some needy people I had never met. But I wasn't doing a thing for my dad, who was such a broken-down piece of a man. I decided it was time to grow up and get over my bitterness. I needed to forgive him. So I got up my nerve and went to see him.

Before long, we had a standing date. Every other week we met at Long John Silver's and shared a fish dinner. Then we started seeing each other every week. The more contact I had with my dad, the more I realized how needy he was. He was always getting beat up, bumming money off people, and being evicted from his apartments. At one of our dinner meetings at Long John Silver's I asked him if he would consider moving in with me if I built two more rooms onto the bar. To my surprise he took me up on it.

It took a month to build the rooms, which I furnished with a TV, VCR, and some nice cots. My dad thought it was absolutely the greatest place he had ever lived. He said to me, "Why did you do this?" And I told him I just wanted to make him happy.

After that we became very close. It was great to talk about our mutual love of baseball and the team I owned. Every time I walked into Dad's rooms he would try to feed me ice cream or grapes or something else from his refrigerator. Gradually, I began to see a different side of him, his generosity and warmth. Despite various barroom brawls, I knew he wouldn't hurt a flea if he could help it. Every Thanksgiving he used to cook a huge meal for any of his customers who had no place to go. And he was always generous with the poor. Once I let go of my resentments, I began to see my dad in a different light.

Shortly after he moved in, I had a dream that really scared me. I saw smoke and total chaos, a place full of ugliness and fear. In the dream I kept descending into the smoke. Further down and further down, the place seemed bottomless. I knew what I was seeing and it terrified me. The worst thing about the dream was that it seemed to represent a kind of judgment on my dad.

I was so frightened when I woke up that I rushed downstairs, relieved to find him sleeping peacefully. That dream really accelerated my prayers and my talks with my dad about God's love and his need for him.

Four months after Dad moved in with me, he suffered a fall and I took him to the hospital. A few days later, the doctor told me Dad had cancer and a weak heart. He might live another three months, but that was all. In fact, my father died of a heart attack that very day.

During his brief stay in the hospital, Dad actually did seem to make his peace with God. He received communion and even talked with my two brothers, who were reconciled to him before he died.

In the funeral home, I knelt before the coffin with my brothers, Stanley Jr. and Dennis. Nobody else was in the room. Despite our problems with Dad, the three of us were heartbroken. As far as we were concerned, he had always been the boss. No matter how often he messed up, we still loved him. His word was always final. Now the boss was dead.

As I looked at my dad in the coffin I couldn't believe what I saw. For a moment, it looked like he was smiling.

When we left the room, my older brother, Stanley, turned to me and said: "Did you see that?" I hadn't imagined it. Both of us had noted the smile on Dad's face. I couldn't help but think it was God's way of letting us know that he too loved this stubborn old man and that he was watching out for him.

I was grateful for my dream, even though it frightened me. It had warned me about Dad's death and about his spiritual condition, and it lessened the shock of losing him so suddenly. More than that it gave me the courage to talk to Dad about getting right with God before it was too late. I could live with myself, knowing I had done my best to be a good son to him. I loved him, and I knew the boss loved me.

Reunited

*T*erri Youngsma lives in California with her three boys, Derek, Nicholas, and Cory. She runs a dental lab out of her home, producing orthodontic study models for local dentists. In early 1994, her husband, Wayne, had a dream about his older brother, Jeff, who had died of cancer the year before. Looking back, Terri wonders if Wayne's dream wasn't God's way of preparing them both for his own death six months later.

꒷

I was working late one night when Wayne came into the kitchen, pale, shaking, and sweaty. He was having a severe insulin reaction, and his eyes looked wild. A lifelong diabetic, he said he needed some sugar.

Once Wayne calmed down, he told me about the dream he had just had. In his dream, the doorbell had rung. When he opened the door, his brother Jeff was standing there. Neither of them spoke. They just hugged each other in the entryway, so glad to be together again.

"I know how much you miss him," I said, aware of how depressed he had been since his brother's death.

"Yes, I do, but this was real. It was just like you and I are talking right now. I saw Jeff," he insisted.

This dream was so vivid that it had actually triggered an insulin reaction. It happened six months before the day I will never forget.

It was September 28, 1994. At 7:00 A.M. I kissed Wayne good-bye just as I had every other morning of our seventeen years together. He assured me he would get home from work in time to take Cory to baseball practice that night.

Once I got the kids off to school, I decided to finish my coffee outside on the patio. I rarely took the time to enjoy such a leisurely moment, but the sunrise was especially gorgeous that day, lending a golden hue to the surrounding orange groves and the mountains beyond.

As I savored the view, I began to sense something was terribly wrong. But how could anything be wrong in the midst of such a peaceful scene? Suddenly, it seemed as though God put a thought into my head: "Just as the sunrise is different each morning, each day is different. You don't know what the day holds, but I want you to know I am here and I am in control."

Believe me, I am not the kind of person who says God told me this or that. I was startled by what I had heard.

At 9:00 A.M. I got a phone call from the San Bernardino County Medical Center. My heart started pounding furiously. "Do you know a Wayne Youngsma?"

"What's wrong?" I asked. The voice on the other end of the line was silent for a moment.

"Ma'am, you need to come over here right away."

As soon as I reached the medical center, I knew the worst had happened. Wayne had suffered a heart attack on the way to work and had died instantly in a high-speed rollover. A driver behind him had seen him slumped over the wheel. When the road curved, Wayne's truck kept going straight.

It's still hard for me to talk about Wayne's death. I miss him so. But Wayne's dream about his brother Jeff and my experience on the patio six months later, the day my husband died, have been a tremendous comfort.

Wayne was only forty when he died. Afterward, I wondered if his dream about Jeff had been a sign they would soon be together again. Both brothers had been terribly close. Both had become Christians shortly before Jeff's death at age forty-nine.

Hard as his death was on me and the kids, I couldn't help thanking God for his mercy toward Wayne. He'd had diabetes since he was fourteen. His blood pressure was very high, and the disease had ravaged his body, resulting in kidney damage. It was all Wayne could do to make it through a day's work. As soon as he got home, Wayne would take a nap on the couch. I would wake him for dinner, and then he would go back to bed for the rest of the evening. I was grateful he hadn't needed to suffer for a prolonged period of time.

After Wayne's death, I thought about what had happened the night before Jeff died. Wayne had been with him that evening. His brother was in a lot of pain but he kept saying, "There's a staircase in my room. What's a stairway doing here?" Of course, Wayne couldn't see anything, but Jeff kept insisting. It made me wonder.

For my part, I know our lives lead somewhere. No one can convince me that everything ends when our hearts stop beating and we take our last breath. I like to think about Jeff heading up those stairs with Wayne right behind him. It helps me to know they are together again.

Seven

❧

Beckoning Dreams

*Once my heart was captured, reason was shown the door,
deliberately and with a sort of frantic joy. I accepted everything,
I believed everything, without struggle, without suffering, without regret,
without false shame. How can one blush for what one adores?*
—GEORGE SAND

any people recognize the story of Monica and Augustine, but few know about the dream she had prior to his conversion. It couldn't have been easy for the mother of such a brilliantly wayward son to keep hoping and praying he would have a change of heart. Augustine had been living with his mistress, with whom he had fathered a child. Reading his *Confessions* is like reading the story of a modern-day man who had been addicted to sexual pleasure. Furthermore, he had rejected Christianity in favor of the Manichaean heresy, popular at the time. Augustine recounts Monica's dream in the *Confessions*:

> She dreamed that she was standing on a wooden rule, and coming towards her in a halo of splendor she saw a young man who smiled at her in joy, although she herself was sad and quite consumed with grief. He asked her the reason for her sorrow and her daily tears, not because he did not know, but because he had something to tell her, for this is what happens in visions. When she replied that her tears were for the soul I had lost, he told her to take heart for, if she looked carefully, she would see that where she was there also was I. And when she looked, she saw me standing beside her on the same rule.... The dream had given new spirit to her hope.

Gregory of Nazianzen was a leader of the church in the fourth century who ascribed his faith to dreams he had had since boyhood. One of his dreams, he said, "was the hidden spark that set his whole life aflame for God."

At the age of sixteen, a boy named Patrick was kidnapped in Britain by Irish pirates and taken to Ireland, where he worked for six years as a shepherd. He had a dream that brought his captivity to an end.

One night he heard a voice in a dream assuring him that a ship stood ready to carry him home to his country. Despite the fact that he was two hundred miles from the coast, the young Patrick decided to heed the dream and flee his captors. Just as the dream had foretold, he found a ship that conveyed him safely to Britain. Later, Patrick described the calm he felt during his escape: "I came in the power of God who was guiding my way for a good purpose and I had no fear all the time until I reached the ship."

Years later, Patrick came back a bishop to the land of his captivity and is credited with bringing the Gospel to the Irish. It would probably have astonished the fifth-century Patrick to think that centuries later thousands of Irishmen would celebrate his achievements with a toast of green beer every March 17.

John Newton is remembered for penning the hymn "Amazing Grace." Few people know that he was a slave trader and a hard-driving seaman before his conversion to Christianity, which began with a dream. Newton dreamed he was on deck of a ship docked in the harbor of Venice. A man approached and offered him a ring, which he quickly accepted. Before departing, the man told him that the ring would bring him great happiness were he to keep it safe. But lose it and he would know great misery.

A second man soon took the place of the first. This man asked about the ring on Newton's finger. When Newton explained the value of the ring, the man scoffed and urged him to toss it overboard. In the dream, Newton plucked the ring from his finger and threw it into the water. The moment the ring touched the water, the mountains around the harbor burst into flames. The man who had urged him to discard the ring derided Newton for his foolishness, telling him he must now follow him to the burning mountains.

Newton wrote: "I trembled, and was in great agony."

But the dream hadn't ended. Newton met a third man, who asked him why he was so sad. When he explained how he had foolishly discarded the ring, the man asked whether he would be wiser should the ring be returned to him. Before Newton could respond, the third man leapt into the water and retrieved the ring. As he climbed back aboard ship, the flames of the mountains were extinguished.

Newton was disturbed by the dream for two or three days but didn't think about it again until several years later, when, in his words, "I found myself in circumstances very nearly resembling those suggested by this extraordinary dream, when I stood helpless and hopeless upon the brink of an awful eternity."

Twenty years after the dream, John Newton, ex-seaman and slave trader, entered the ministry. No wonder he penned these words as part of his most famous hymn:

> Through many dangers, toils, and snares,
>   I have already come,
> 'Tis grace has brought me safe thus far,
>   And grace will lead me home.

A dream had foreshadowed the path his life would take.

Lilias Trotter was a Christian missionary who lived in Algeria in the early years of the twentieth century. She recounts the story of a dream, told to her by a Muslim woman who had converted to Christianity:

Blind Houriya came this morning with "I want to tell you something that has frightened me very much. I dreamed it Saturday night, but I was too frightened to tell you yesterday. Today my husband told me, 'You must tell.' I dreamed that a great snake was twisting round my throat and strangling me. I called to you but you said: 'I cannot save you, for you are not following our road.' I went on calling for help, and one came up to me and loosened the snake from off my neck. I said: 'And who is it that is saving me, and what is this snake?' A voice said: 'I am Jesus. . . .'"

Dreams can connect the natural world with the supernatural. They can reach beyond our defenses and help us make our choice. Dreams can show us the emptiness of a life bereft of God—if we listen. Let us listen to the stories that follow.

The Dream of the Golden Fish

*A*s one writer has said, "Trying to figure out what Eric Metaxas is going to do next is like sticking a pushpin into a cyclone." A graduate of Yale, Eric is the former editorial director for Rabbit Ears Productions, where he wrote scripts for children's audio and video products narrated by the likes of Mel Gibson, Robin Williams, and Michael Keaton. An award-winning author who cut his literary teeth in the prestigious Yaddo and McDowell writing colonies, Eric's writing has appeared in such venues as the *New York Times Sunday Magazine* and *Atlantic Monthly*. In recent years, he has written screenplays, sitcom scripts, short fiction, humor books, and children's books. In 1988 he had a dream which symbolized a new beginning in his life.

I have always loved to fish, especially in winter. I particularly liked ice fishing. For me, it was a thrill to dangle bait in the dark, cool waters and then, bang, to thread a living creature through the small opening, from one side of the frozen world to the next.

So it is hardly surprising that this image of a frozen lake took on a more symbolic meaning for me while I was an undergraduate at Yale, searching for answers to the meaning of life.

I should probably begin by saying that I am the son of Greek Orthodox parents. When I was a child, my father would point to bumper stickers displaying a fish symbol and explain that the early Christians used the fish as a secret symbol for Christ because the Greek word for fish, *ichthys*, is an acronym for "Jesus Christ, the Son of God our Savior." So the image of a fish was important to me, even as a young child.

Still, I was never more than nominal when it came to matters of faith. At Yale, I began to search for some kind of grand synthesis, a scheme or system that would encapsulate and express the purpose and meaning of life. I had read a bit of Freud and Jung and was fascinated by their ideas about the unconscious. It seemed to me that what other people called "God" was actually the collective unconscious—the wild, unpredictable, hidden side of the human personality. The more I read, the more I began to develop an image in my mind. I envisioned a frozen lake in which the ice represented the conscious mind and the water beneath it, the unconscious. The point and purpose of life was to drill through the conscious part in order to reach the unconscious. Once this was done, the ice would be transformed into a permeable membrane connecting the worlds of the conscious and the unconscious, and bang, you'd be a whole, healthy person—reconciled to yourself, as it were.

My career beyond Yale looked rather bright. An English major, I had won two of the most coveted senior prizes for fiction. I foolishly expected to be published in the *New Yorker* and to have written a successful novel by the age of twenty-three or twenty-four. It didn't happen that way. Instead, in the space of three years, I sold two humor pieces to the *Atlantic Monthly* and a short story to another magazine— hardly enough to pay the rent and stock the refrigerator, let alone achieve new heights of literary brilliance. Despite my aspirations, I fit the portrait of the starving artist rather well: I was barely surviving, frustrated, and depressed.

In 1987 I moved back home so I could sort out what I was going to do next. After graduating from Yale, my immigrant parents had expected me to have the world by the tail. They had little patience with a twenty-four-year-old son "searching for himself," who had no money, no career, and few prospects. I couldn't imagine things getting worse. Which only illustrated how limited my imagination could be.

Desperate for work, I accepted a position at Union Carbide as a proofreader. The job was utter torture. I was approximately a tenth of a mile from the nearest window, and I thought I would lose my mind, spending endless hours poring over manuals with nothing but column after column of numbers.

While I was at Union Carbide, I made friends with a coworker who was a devout Christian—Episcopalian actually. I had known several Episcopalians at Yale, and they seemed safe enough. So I started asking him questions that had been bothering me, questions about the meaning of life and my place in it. We started having lunch together fairly regularly, and he would tell me about his own deep faith. Still, I was wary. I didn't want to go overboard with this religious stuff. But I began praying, rather halfheartedly, that God would reveal himself to me if, in fact, he actually existed.

Soon after, I had a dream that I was ice fishing on Candlewood Lake, near my home in Danbury, Connecticut. It was one of those absolutely glorious winter days where the sun is low and intensely golden and bright and the sky is an amazing blue. As I was peering into the hole chopped in the ice, I reached down and pulled out the most beautiful fish I'd ever seen—a bronze-colored pike that was more than two feet long. As I lifted it, though, to look at it, the sun shone on it making it look gold, and then I realized that no, it actually was gold. It was a golden fish. And it was alive.

In the dream I knew that the fish was Christ—I just knew right away, and as I held this golden fish to my breast I knew that it was over, the painful search, the struggle, the depression. He'd come to me, just as I'd prayed he would. He was in my arms now and he was mine and I was filled with this amazing joy—and I was just beaming.

The next day, I confided my dream to my friend at work. When he asked what I thought it meant, I told him I knew that it meant I had accepted Jesus. It was over. I was no longer searching, no longer alone, no longer praying to a God who might not exist. And as I told him that, the same joy that erupted inside me in the dream filled me again. I'll never forget it.

What especially amazes me is that I had simply wanted to drill a hole through the ice, to pierce the conscious world in order to reach the unconscious. But God had actually one-upped me: he had decided to create an opening in my soul, so to speak, to forge a connection between the natural world and the supernatural. And out of this place between two worlds he would allow me to draw the gift of a living, golden fish, the gift of his Son. The identical dream could have been given to someone else and it would have meant nothing. But God, in order to communicate his love, chose to use images intensely personal and meaningful to me and me alone.

That dream was the turning point of my life. It no longer mattered that I hadn't yet achieved my dreams of becoming a writer. I actually didn't care whether I had to stay in a dead-end job for the rest of my life. No kidding. I just wanted to be wherever God wanted me in order to accomplish whatever he wanted me to do. As it turns out, he did have other plans for me. But that's another story.

"I Dreamed about a Man
I Never Met"

$\mathcal{H}$ayward Sparks and his wife, Karen, live in Ann Arbor, Michigan. Hayward owns a thriving insurance business and has been featured in ads in *Black Enterprise* because of the success he has gained in his profession. Four years ago, he had a dream about a man he has never met who lives in a town he didn't even know existed.

෴

I've never been big on dreams. That's why it surprised me when I began to wonder whether God might be trying to catch my attention through some of mine. At times I would have a dream, forget about it, and then watch it come true in the real world.

For instance, Susan was a friend of ours who was expecting to deliver a child in a few weeks. She was working and still had a lot to do to get ready for the baby. One night I had a dream we were both at the same party. In my dream, I walked up to her and said, "Susan, you better get ready. You need to wrap things up because nothing's going to stop that baby from coming. It's going to be here this Friday." That Sunday I saw her at church and told her about the dream. Susan did what I probably would have. She laughed and said the doctor had told her she wasn't due for three more weeks. Not to worry, she had plenty of time. But guess what—that baby showed up the next Friday.

That dream and others like it began to make me think and pray more about my dreams. As I did so, I began to get a feel for which of them were caused by indigestion and which were worth taking more seriously.

Not long afterward, I had a dream that I was on television interviewing a man by the name of Oscar L. Lennon Jr. (not the real name). I could see him clearly. He was a black man with a thin neck, whose shirts were too large. I was holding a microphone and asking him about how he came to have such a great relationship with God. I can't remember much about his answers, but we had a pleasant conversation, very warm and encouraging. Draped behind us was a big white banner with black letters spelling out the word "Reading."

When I woke up, I told my wife, Karen, about the dream and asked if she had ever heard of a place called "Reading." She's from Erie, Pennsylvania, and so she thought right away about Reading, Pennsylvania, though she explained that it was pronounced "Redding." We got out the map, and sure enough, there it was, northwest of Philadelphia.

"Well, however you pronounce it, I think I'm supposed to call this Oscar L. Lennon Jr. and tell him that Someone up above is very interested in him." But the whole thing was so outlandish—I just blew it off. I went to work and didn't even think about it.

But Karen brought it up at dinner that night. "You know, honey," she said, "God has been speaking to you in your dreams and you better do something about this one. Even if you find this guy, he won't know who you are, so what do you have to lose?"

Her argument made sense, so I dialed the number for information in Reading, Pennsylvania, and the operator told me there were several Lennon's listed, even one Oscar L. Lennon. But it wasn't Oscar

L. Lennon Jr. so I kept pressing for more listings. Finally she checked a nearby town with the same area code. Sure enough, there was an Oscar L. Lennon Jr.! Well, by now I was so amazed that the hair on my neck was standing up. I dialed the number and a girl answered.

"You don't know me," I said. "My name is Hayward Sparks and I'm from Ann Arbor, Michigan. I know this is going to sound crazy, but I had a dream about someone named Oscar L. Lennon Jr., and I wonder if he lives there."

"Yes, I'm his daughter," she said.

I told her the dream and she was silent for a few moments. Then she said, "Hold on a minute. Let me go get my mother." When her mother got on the phone I explained it all over again. I told her I had seen a man with a thin neck and oversized shirt in my dream. I described his complexion and the way he wore his hair. Did that sound like her husband?

"Yes, that's Oscar," she said.

When I finished retelling the dream, she said, "I've been praying for something to happen for my husband so that he could really believe in God. He's been down and out on his luck lately, and he really needs God. But he won't listen to me about this. He's not here right now, but this is such an answer to prayer."

I gave her my phone number in case he wanted to call when he got in. About an hour later the phone rang and the man I had only dreamed about and never met was on the other end of the line. Oscar was very quiet as I told him about the dream and shared my faith. You know, I don't think there were any flashing lights or that he fell down on his knees and thanked God or anything like that, but I could tell by his voice he was very emotional. I knew the dream had touched him in a very deep place.

To this day, I don't know the end of this story. That's between this man and God. But I am certain of one thing. God knows where each of us lives—the state, the county, the city, the neighborhood, the street, the color of the house, the number on the door. He knows who we are and what makes us tick. He knows us better than we know ourselves. And he always comes calling. Of that I am sure.

Dreams That Marked the Journey

*B*ob Hartig is a copywriter for a large publishing company. He grew up in the Midwest and was reared in a church-going family. In junior high school he had his first brush with the occult. It would be years of spiritual struggle before he would emerge with any kind of clarity about what he believed and where he was headed. He tells a little of his spiritual journey to highlight the significance of dreams he received at two very different stages in that journey.

༈

Believe me, I didn't go looking for the occult. It came looking for me. I was in junior high when I had my first encounter with it. I was a good enough kid back then and certainly wouldn't have qualified as a rebellious teenager. In fact, an instructor in my Christian education class was the one who opened the door to evil and ushered me through it—along with several other kids.

One night we actually conducted a séance, holding hands and calling on the devil. It was an eerie experience and one that scared most of us silly. I don't know how many nights after that I kept a Bible under my pillow—the only thing I knew that might shield me from the fear.

A few years later, I landed in the middle of another unusual spiritual scene. But this time it was by choice. I had made friends with people who were involved in the occult and was interested in learning whatever they could teach me. I was fifteen and hanging out at a local ashram. One of the mahatmas was to deliver a "divine discourse" at a nearby college. As followers, we were there to listen and learn from the teaching of the guru. But as soon as the mahatma stopped talking, a group of Jesus people began refuting his words. One of them approached me. He didn't tell me I was wrong but simply said, "Just be very, very careful about what you're doing."

For whatever reason, this man's words became like a burr inside my soul. I began to question whether I was on the right track. By then I realized there was such a thing as false light, a spiritual path that seems true but is actually deceptive. The people at the ashram told me simply to pray to the little guru in my heart and he would guide me. But I wasn't sure—and I wanted to be sure. So I prayed to a God I did not know and asked him to reveal himself.

God answered my prayer in ways that convinced me of the reality of Christ. But I didn't see why I couldn't keep smoking dope and getting drunk as I always had. I figured I could party whenever I wanted as long as I asked Jesus to save me. Then I had a dream that put things in a different light.

I was eighteen at the time it happened. I'd been out that night with a friend and returned home pretty well lubricated. In my dream, my friend and I were still driving down the road when I noticed to our right a cloud over the hilltops, shaped like a cross and glowing intensely. When I looked again, I saw a second glowing cloud with a man's hand sticking out of it, pointing skyward. We continued barreling down the road in the car . . . and then I saw a man standing in the sky. He too was shining brilliantly. He didn't say anything—just stared straight at me intently.

Even though I was driving in my dream, I tried to roll down the window, hoping I could squeeze through it and run toward the man in the sky. In the dream I was laughing though I suddenly found myself thinking, "Geez, I'm drunk. What's he going to think? Here he is just staring at me." Then I woke up.

Looking back, the dream scene reminded me of the description in the book of Revelation: "His eyes were like blazing fire. His feet were like bronze glowing in a furnace. . . . His face was like the sun shining in all its brilliance." Nothing before nor since has approached the brightness of that dream. To put it less eloquently, it was like looking up and seeing an incandescent lightbulb in the sky.

I really believe that Jesus appeared to me in that dream. It was like a preaching of the Gospel. Even though it touched me deeply, the dream didn't affect my behavior right away. It was like a slow-growing seed that took root inside me.

Another dream came to me several years later, after I had become more serious about my faith. This one wasn't as dramatic, but it helped encourage and guide me through a difficult time.

Before I describe the dream, I should mention that years ago I developed the habit of walking along a set of railroad tracks in order to be alone with God. As I walk, I read from a pocket Bible, memorizing and meditating on Scripture. This is my outdoor sanctuary, a place where I experience God's touch. Here's what happened in my dream.

I was watching a television movie about a man who was raising crops on railroad tracks. As I watched the documentary, the television set disappeared and the man on the screen began walking toward me, large as life, with fields of wheat rising behind him wherever he stepped. It was like watching Johnny Appleseed stride across the country with apple trees growing up behind him.

I looked at him and said, "What's the secret of your success?" The man stared at me and replied in a gruff voice, "You just got to get out there and do it." That was it. I woke up.

Before the dream, I had been questioning my fruitfulness as a Christian, wondering if my prayers were having an effect. The dream seemed to be God's way of reassuring me that the times I'd spent seeking his face, pouring my heart out to him in prayer had not been wasted. He wanted me to know the seeds I planted would bear fruit and that I needed to keep on sowing and keep on watering. The dream reassured me I really was on the "right track."

Because of my background, I am only too aware that a person can have all kinds of spiritual experiences and still not be in a safe place. Though I hunger for the touch of God, I don't believe that dreams or supernatural experiences are always from him. It takes wisdom to tell the difference between what comes from him, from our imagination, or from evil itself. More than a supernatural experience, I hunger for the truth, because that's what has changed my life so dramatically.

Fire in the Desert

*M*ary McDermott Shideler is the author of numerous books, including *Theology of Romantic Love: A Study of the Writings of Charles Williams, Consciousness of Battle*, and her newest, *Starting Out*. The daughter of a federal judge, she describes herself as having been a difficult child, whose imaginative, intuitive personality clashed with her parents' more legalistic approach to life. More than sixty years ago, at the age of sixteen, she had a dream that confirmed her intimations of a transcendent spiritual reality. Like a story, a picture, a dance, it appealed to her imagination rather than to her intellect and therefore communicated more than it explicitly said.

~

The dream occurred in the early morning of July 22, 1933. I was sixteen years old.

I was crossing a desert of red sand and red rocks, under a red sky. The footing must have been rough because I remember my relief at a moment's rest when I came to a comparatively clear space. I knew that around me others were trudging in the same direction. Where we were going, why we were there, I did not know. In silence we simply plodded on.

After a time, I was on the ledge of a cliff overlooking the red plain. A visible flame moved from one person to another but not to all. It seemed to pick an erratic course, and I knew that it was coming next to me.

I waited for it because there was nothing else I could do. Even had I not been paralyzed by terror, there was no place on that narrow ledge for me to go. It approached. It reached me and I was swept by an intense heat that burned me without pain. It engulfed me, and I endured it in that eternity which is without beginning or end or duration. Simultaneously, I was utterly annihilated and utterly fulfilled beyond any possibility of description. When it had gone, I held gold in my hand.

I woke speaking words that had been given me: "Gold from dross."

Was it a dream or a vision? Was it the product of psychological tensions deep in my subconscious, or a revelation from God? Later, when I came across the writings of the mystics, I recognized instantly that my dream differed from the classic mystical experience only in that it had occurred, or had begun, when I was asleep.

In the dream, I had felt as if I were being approached by something beyond and alien to myself, an Other. While psychologists could offer a coherent and persuasive explanation of my experience, the explanation of the mystics was equally coherent and persuasive. The alternatives implied different doctrines and carried different consequences for living. Through the years I was drawn down and down to the one point: what had come to me in the dream—God or my unconscious self? Had I been confronted with something outside or inside myself? And how, in heaven's name, could I tell?

In the end, I decided God had met me there. I did not choose that alternative because it solved more of my problems. If anything, it raised more since it set me in opposition to the world in which I had been brought up and which still surrounded me. Not because it offered a simpler rationale for living. On the contrary, by isolating me from my fellows, it created complications of many kinds. Not because it saved me from the judgment that my innermost self was a sinkhole and my actions the result of despicable motives. If the dream were from God, his judgment—as expressed in the annihilatory aspect of the dream—was even more terrible. Instead, my choice was made on the only ground which in the end can be held and defended with complete integrity: that one alternative rang true, and the other did not.

It was left to me to accept or reject the Presence in my dream. Only by a shred, a whisper, the splitting of a hair, I chose the rending joy of heaven over the pursuit of pleasure, belief over unbelief, fulfillment over success. And I have never regretted that choice.

"I Dreamed of a Golden City"

*R*arely are we in a position to interpret the dreams of others. Most often, the dreamer needs to validate the meaning of the dream in his or her own life. But sometimes the dreamer may need help interpreting a significant dream.

A graduate of Yale University, Paul Thigpen is the author of thirteen books and is assistant professor of religious studies at Southwest Missouri State University. On tour in Europe during the 1970s with the Yale University Glee Club, Paul heard the story of a piercingly beautiful dream, confided to him by a fellow student. He has never forgotten it.

⌀

Mark and I had become good friends during our summer tour of Europe. He was a nice Jewish kid from New York who knew so little about his religious heritage that he wouldn't have recognized Moses if he spotted him strolling through the Red Sea. And while he knew next-to-nothing about the Old Testament, his knowledge of Jesus and the New Testament was simply nonexistent.

One day, Mark had a severe allergic reaction to something in the air—for him a frequent problem. Though he carried medicine with him in the event of an attack, he usually had to get emergency medical treatment if he didn't take the medicine quickly enough. This time, as he began to choke up and worried aloud that he might need a doctor, I offered to pray for him and he said yes. Remarkably, the reaction subsided. That experience must have impressed him, because one morning he came to me and said, "Paul, I've had a dream and I believe you're the one who's supposed to interpret it." I was studying religion at Yale, not dream interpretation, but I told him I'd be glad to listen.

"In my dream," he explained, "I was standing with a friend looking up into the sky and in the sky was a beautiful golden city. As soon as we saw it, we knew we wanted to get there. But we didn't know how. Suddenly, we saw a tree that seemed to be engulfed in flames. It kept burning but it wasn't consumed. We got the idea that if we could climb that tree, we could reach the golden city. But whenever we tried, we were forced to give up because the fire was so intense. We fell back and began to cry and tell each other we would never get there. But then I heard a voice that seemed to come from above us. It was the sound of a man groaning in pain, and I knew he was dying, and the strangest thing is that I also knew he was God. But how could someone be both man and God, and if he was God how could he be dying, I kept asking myself. When the groaning stopped, I knew the man was dead, and suddenly I thought that maybe we could make it to that golden city after all. But as we approached the tree, I heard another voice saying, 'Not until the morning of the third day.'

"Paul, none of this makes any sense to me. Do you know what it means?"

I was so astonished by the dream that I blurted out: "Well, you're Jewish, aren't you? Don't you know the story of Moses and the burning bush?" He didn't.

"The Old Testament," I explained, "tells how God appeared to Moses in a bush that burned without burning up. The burning bush represents the presence of God. And Scripture talks about the golden city being the kingdom of heaven waiting for us. But we can't make it there on our own efforts because we lack holiness. In your dream, the fire in the tree represents the holiness of God. Without being purified, the fire would destroy us before we reached heaven."

"But what about the man who was also God?" he asked.

"Don't you know that Christians believe Jesus was both man and God and that he was crucified?" He didn't.

"Christians believe," I continued, "that Jesus had to die on a cross—a tree—before the way would be open for us to heaven. Furthermore, the gospel story tells us that Jesus was lifeless until the morning of the third day when he rose from the dead and later ascended to the Father, opening the gate of heaven for us."

Mark looked at me wide-eyed all the time I was speaking. Despite asking me to interpret his dream, he was astonished it made sense to me. After that we lost touch, and I don't know what became of him. But I do know one thing: that dream came from a source totally beyond Mark. While he was sleeping, God lifted the curtain between heaven and earth so that Mark would one day have a chance to reach the city in his dream.

Thy thoughts of love are so many that my mind never gets away from them, they surround me at all hours. I go to my bed, and God is my last thought; and when I awake I find my mind still hovering about His palace gates. God is ever with me, and I am ever with Him. This is life indeed. If during my sleep my mind wanders away into dreams, yet it only wanders upon holy ground, and the moment I wake my heart is back with the Lord.

—CHARLES SPURGEON

$\mathcal{S}$OURCES ॐ

Page 14: Reynolds Price in Naomi Epel, *Writers Dreaming* (New York: Random House, 1993), 202.

Page 14: Kelly Bulkeley, *Spiritual Dreaming: A Cross-cultural and Historical Journey* (New York: Paulist, 1995), 156.

Page 17: Charles Haddon Spurgeon, as quoted in James Ryle, *A Dream Come True* (Orlando, Fla.: Creation House), 25.

Page 17: John Calvin, as quoted in James Ryle, *A Dream Come True*, 205.

Page 18: Maya Angelou in Naomi Epel, *Writers Dreaming*, 29.

Page 23: George Howe Colt, "The Power of Dreams," *Life* magazine (September 1995), 46.

Page 27: Bill McCartney as quoted in Ryle, *A Dream Come True*, 8–9.

Page 28: As cited in Ryle, *A Dream Come True*, 49–50.

Page 28: As cited in Robert L. Van de Castle, *Our Dreaming Mind* (New York: Ballantine, 1994), 25.

Page 29: Van de Castle, *Our Dreaming Mind*, 28–29.

Page 30: Van de Castle, *Our Dreaming Mind*, 30.

Page 30: Van de Castle, *Our Dreaming Mind*, 26–27.

Page 31: Van de Castle, *Our Dreaming Mind*, 32–33.

Page 31: Ryle, *A Dream Come True*, 137.

Page 31: Paul Meier and Robert Wise, *Windows of the Soul: A Look at Dreams and Their Meaning* (Nashville: Thomas Nelson, 1995), 170–71.

Page 52: Ryle, *A Dream Come True*, 127–29.

Page 53: Van de Castle, *Our Dreaming Mind*, 26.

Page 53: Van de Castle, *Our Dreaming Mind*, 22.

Page 76: Van de Castle, *Our Dreaming Mind*, 364.

Page 76: Carl G. Jung, *Man and His Symbols* (New York: Dell, 1964), 66.

Page 76: Van de Castle, *Our Dreaming Mind*, 373.

Page 77: Van de Castle, *Our Dreaming Mind*, 373.

Page 77: Van de Castle, *Our Dreaming Mind*, 394–95.

Page 78: Van de Castle, *Our Dreaming Mind*, 363–64.

Page 92: Louis M. Savary, Patricia H. Berne, and Strephon Kaplan Williams, *Dreams and Spiritual Growth* (New York: Paulist Press, 1984), 55–56.

Page 93: Jeremy Taylor, *Dream Work: Techniques for Discovering the Creative Power in Dreams* (New York: Paulist, 1983), 7.

Page 93: Van de Castle, *Our Dreaming Mind*, 15.

Page 117: Ryle, *A Dream Come True*, 156.

Page 117: Bulkeley, *Spiritual Dreaming*, 81.

Page 118: David Fontana, *The Secret Language of Dreams* (San Francisco: Chronicle, 1994), 21.

Page 144: As quoted in Bulkeley, *Spiritual Dreaming*, 111.

Page 144: Bulkeley, *Spiritual Dreaming*, 136.

Page 145: Ryle, *A Dream Come True*, 163.

Page 146: As quoted in Bulkeley, *Spiritual Dreaming*, 20.

A Miracle a Day: Stories of Heavenly Encounters
ANN SPANGLER

Anyone who has ever longed for a miracle will take heart from the remarkable true stories in *A Miracle a Day*.

Here's what you can look forward to ...

A schoolgirl is healed of bulbar polio, a man is miraculously pulled from a burning wreck, a young child finds a lost diamond ring, a woman on the brink of death receives a vision of heaven, an angel takes a young girl on the trip of a lifetime. True stories from Scripture and from the lives of ordinary men and women as well as such notable figures as Catherine Marshall, Briege McKenna, John Newton, Francis of Assisi, and General George Patton open a window into the miracles that will reassure you that God still loves you and is in control of the universe.

A Miracle a Day is a book of fifty-five devotions that reflect on God's incredible love, exploring such themes as miracles of healing, miracles of deliverance, miracles of prophecy, miracles and angels, the power of prayer when miracles don't happen, and the significance of dreams and visions.

No matter what your need, *A Miracle a Day* will deepen your faith in the wisdom, kindness, and mercy of an all-powerful God.

A Miracle a Day: Stories of Heavenly Encounters
0-310-20794-0 - Hardcover

We want to hear from you. Please send your comments about this
book to us in care of the address below. Thank you.

ZondervanPublishingHouse
Grand Rapids, Michigan 49530
http://www.zondervan.com